CITY
PLANNING
HOW CITIZENS CAN TAKE CONTROL

CONNOR MURPHY

City Planning: How Citizens Can Take Control

Published by Wheatmark®
2030 East Speedway Boulevard, Suite 106
Tucson, Arizona 85719 USA
www.wheatmark.com

ISBN: 978-1-62787-881-4
ISBN: 978-1-62787-882-1
LCCN: 2021905431

Bulk ordering discounts are available through Wheatmark, Inc. For more information, email orders@wheatmark.com or call 1-888-934-0888.

for Paige

CONTENTS

Chapter 1
INTRODUCTION TO CITY PLANNING

Every time you decide to do something or go somewhere, you are planning. Planning can be as simple as making a list.

Whenever you decide to go somewhere, first you visualize your goal and then you let your mind fill in the steps to getting there. Planning is so automatic that you don't even realize you're doing it. When you say, "I'm going to the store," you automatically plot out the path as you walk out the door. The next thing you know, you're at the store. But many city plans go astray—they don't reach their goal. I wrote this book to explain how ordinary folks like yourself can make sure that your local city plan reaches its goal.

TARGET AUDIENCE-ORDINARY PEOPLE

There are two ways to do city planning: turn your city over to professional planners and let them decide what is best for you; or take responsibility for deciding what you want your city to be like in the future.

If you want to take responsibility for your city, you have to learn how to actively participate in writing the plan. And in this book, I will explain to you how to do that.

So, welcome to city planning. I hope you enjoy the journey and learn enough to hold your own at planning workshops. My goal is to show you how to participate without getting buffaloed by smooth-talking planners out to promote their own favorite planning concepts. You need to end up with a place where you want to live, not one of those "cities of the future" shown on Google,[1] and favored by many city planners—but not by me.

MANY WAYS TO PLAN A CITY

I graduated from planning school in 1972. Back then, I was told there were many ways to plan a city, and that local people should be in control of the outcome. But those days are over.

Many recent planning books claim there is a "right" way to plan and a "wrong" way to plan. Planning has become dogmatic, and ordinary folks are expected to go along with whatever is currently fashionable among city planners. You and other folks need to determine the outcome of the city planning process, not self-anointed experts.

Contemporary city planning. Over the past half-century, three competing dogmas have come to dominate city planning: New Urbanism, Smart Growth, and Neo-traditionalism. All three, claim credit for coming up with the same design approach.

Eight principles have come to define the foundation of contemporary city planning:
1. Mixed land use.
2. Compact urban design.
3. Variety of housing choices.
4. Walkable neighborhoods.
5. Creating a sense of place.
6. Saving open space, farmland, natural beauty, and critical environments
7. Adding growth to existing urban areas.

8. Provide a variety of transportation.

The eight principles are fine in concept, but when I read books written by some of America's best-known planners, I find they each interpret the principles to suit themselves. City planners seem to have trouble agreeing with one another—and many of them don't seem to connect with the values cherished by ordinary Americans.

The American dream. Merriam-Webster dictionary defines the American dream "as a happy way of living . . . that can be achieved by anyone . . . by working hard and becoming successful—good job, a nice house, two children, and plenty of money."

Some of the best-known city planners don't seem to understand how important the American dream is to ordinary folks. So, they feel free to offer their unappealing alternatives such as telling us we should:

- live in high-rise apartment buildings, located downtown on bus routes;
- commute to work by bicycle;
- get rid of our cars;
- live communally, sharing part of our homes with neighbors; and
- convert our single-family homes into apartments so street people can have a place to live.

But the recommended alternatives fly in the face of our most cherished values. According to The Gallup Poll, 27 percent of us want to live in the countryside.[2] And acording to Charlotte O'Malley of *Builder Magazine*, 80 percent of Americans would prefer to live in single-family homes.[3] So why do so many city planners and architects want to push so many of us into high-density downtown apartments —that's not where most of us want to live?

The pursuit of happiness. Philip Reynolds, Director, Pursuit of

Happiness Project at Emory University, says the Declaration of Independence "conveyed the notion of prosperity and personal well-being, especially a life of peace and the enjoyment of the fruits of one's own labor."[4]

Coercive governance. City planning has drifted away from what the Declaration of Independence calls the pursuit of happiness, in favor of autocracy run by an elite not constitutionally responsible to the people. Coercive city planning can be easily disguised as New Urbanism, Smart Growth, and Neo-traditionalism—good ideas easily subverted by false prophets. Not all social engineering works to society's advantage, and some leads to unintended consequences.

State of Oregon. "In 2019, the Oregon Legislature passed House Bill 2001. . . Under the bill, by June 30, 2022, cities . . . [with] over 25,000 population, must allow people to build duplexes, triplexes, fourplexes, cottage clusters, and townhouses in residential areas."[5]

As cited previously, 80 percent of Americans prefer to live in single-family homes. So why has Oregon taken away single-family zoning. Perhaps it's to appease city planning ideologues besotted with communism.

Minneapolis Minnesota. "As of January 1, 2020, Minneapolis became the first large American city to eliminate single-family zoning. . . Minneapolis sought through these zoning changes to increase the supply of affordable housing citywide, increase the variety of housing options in low-density areas, promote integration, and encourage the development of resource-rich, mixed-income neighborhoods of opportunity."[6] LocalHousingSolutions.org defines resource-rich neighborhoods as those that offer abundant amenities. "[Resource rich] neighborhoods offer access to quality schools and public libraries that set the stage for educational achievement, streets and parks that are free from violence and provide a safe place to play, and fresh and healthy food."[7]

Cutting up single-family homes into apartments won't solve America's poverty problem. America's poverty is the result of the mal-distribution of wealth. The official poverty rate in 2019 was 10.5 percent.[8]

Berkeley, California. "The City Council voted to . . . remove minimum parking requirements for all residential land uses . . ."[9]

Berkeley has a severe shortage of parking places. Residents often have to drive around-and-around searching for a place to park. On "game day," Football fans pay to park their cars in peoples' driveways and side yards. (In 2020, parking in a private driveway cost $225.) But the "People's Republic of Berkeley", rather than responding to the need for parking, Finance Geek tells us, Berkeley has bowed to the Anti-Car Movement:

> "There's an anti-car movement brewing across America. They're well-funded, tech savvy, and politically active. They guise their hatred of cars under pretenses of environmental protection, mass transit, and health, but underneath it's all because they hate the car."[10]

Attack on freedom of choice. I don't know about you, but I don't want Oregon, Minneapolis, Berkeley or any other political body telling me what's best for me. And I don't want some self-anointed expert telling me to give up my own interpretation of the American dream. I believe ordinary folks should have the freedom to stand up for the American dream—"good job, a nice house, two children, and plenty of money."

INVOLVE YOURSELF IN LOCAL GOVERNANCE

S. E. Smith writing in Bustle, has this to say about participation in local planning: "The hands-down number one best way to participate in local politics is to show up at City Council meetings . . . Unfortunately, showing up at government meetings is one of the most painful and annoying experiences on Earth, but you're going to have to suck it up, buttercup — because if you have a problem with . . . local policy issues that impact your day-to-day life, you're going to need to bring your pretty little face to these meetings. Bring your knitting. It helps."[11]

To Smith's words of wisdom, I'll add my own suggestion: One of the easiest ways to get acquainted with city planning is to read one of my other books:

- *Fight City Hall and Win: How to Defend Your Community Against Rapacious Developers, Scared Bureaucrats, and Corrupt Politicians.* The book was specifically written to serve the needs of ordinary folks who need the right tools to take on the powers that be—and win.
- *Common Sense Zoning: Practical Solutions for Smaller Cities.* The book presents land use regulations both professional city planners and ordinary folks can easily understand: Regulations that simplify Euclidian zoning; make sense to people who lack expertise in zoning; clearly explain the decision-making process; invite ordinary people to participate in governance; and regulations that protect communities from scoundrels.

So now let's move on to what you need to know if you want to take responsibility for planning your city.

HISTORICAL CITY PLANNING

Settlers from the Old World brought their city planning concepts with them to America, and immediately upon arrival they started laying out places to live. European-based city planning can be traced back to St. Augustine, Florida, in 1565;[12] the Roanoke Colony, North Carolina, in 1585;[13] and Jamestown, Virginia, in 1607.[14] Native

Americans also planned cities. Cahokia[15] (across the Mississippi from St. Louis) and Chaco Canyon[16] (in New Mexico) are two large settlements that predate European cities by eons.

City planning goes back a long way. Damascus,[17] the oldest continuously inhabited city in the world, dates back at least 11,000 years.

CONTEMPORARY CITY PLANNING

Contemporary city planning in the United States can be traced back to two official federal acts:

- **Standard State Zoning Enabling Act of 1926.**[18] This federal act was a model that states could follow in writing their own zoning regulations. (In my book *Common Sense Zoning: Practical Solutions for Smaller Cities*, I explain what zoning is and how it works.)
- **Standard City Planning Enabling Act of 1928.**[19] This federal act, among other things, addressed control of the private subdivision of land.

City Planning Primer. The Standard City Planning Enabling Act of 1928 has a companion document called the City Planning Primer of 1928.[20] In the forward to the City Planning Primer of 1928, Secretary of Commerce Herbert Hoover had this to say:

"This city planning primer reminds us that city planning is going on about us every day in our cities and towns. Whenever a street is laid out, or a park or school site is acquired, or a home or factory or store is built, someone decides where it is to be located. The planning may be done bit by bit by private land owners and city officials, few of whom know, or can know, what the others are doing or have in mind. Or it may be done by the citizens and their local government working together through a permanent public planning body with a well-devised master plan, which they all use as a picture of how the whole city is developing."[21]

So, since 1928, the federal government has intended for cities to create well-devised master plans that picture the future. The City Planning Primer also emphasizes that orderly development is the objective of the plan and the plan must anticipate probable future needs of the city well in advance of new real estate development. The City Planning Primer lists five physical development aspects that need to be addressed:

Growth trends. The city plan is concerned with "studies of the trend of growth in residential, business, and industrial uses of land and the most desirable directions for such growth."[22]

Transportation. The plan is concerned with "movement of all types to and from the locality and within the locality—major thoroughfares; street railways; bus lines, and other forms of rapid transit; railways, waterways, and harbor developments; and public utility plants, mains, conduits, and wires."[23]

Recreation. The plan is concerned with "recreational facilities, particularly parks, parkways, and playgrounds."[24]

Public facilities. The plan is concerned with "the general location of public buildings of all types, including the city hall, schools, and fire and police stations."[25]

Changing conditions. The plan is concerned with changing conditions. "In a hundred different ways a . . . plan provides for better living conditions, better business, and a more attractive and agreeable [place] in which to live and do business."[26]

INTANGIBLES—ABSTRACT QUALITIES

I believe that it is time to expand the five development aspects from what was included in 1928, so I propose adding four intangible aspects: basic human needs, quality of life, happiness, and seven-generation sustainability.

Basic human needs. American law defines basic human needs as "adequate food, shelter, and clothing plus some household equipment and furniture." Also included are "essential services provided by and for the community-at-large such as safe drinking water, sanitation, health and education."[27]

Quality of life. Quality of life is the expectation of a person to live a good life. It is the overall enjoyment of life—the feeling of general well-being. The Encyclopedia Britannica tells us that "[w]ithin the arena of health care, quality of life is viewed as multidimensional, encompassing emotional, physical, material, and social well-being."[28]

Happiness. The city plan should be concerned with how happy local people are—that is to say, how satisfied and fulfilled they feel.

Seven-Generation Sustainability. According to the philosophy of the Iroquois Confederacy, said to be the oldest living participatory democracy on earth, "In our every deliberation, we must consider the impact of our decisions on the next seven generations. . . . Look and listen for the welfare of the whole people and have always in view not only the present but also the coming generations, even those whose faces are yet beneath the surface of the ground — the unborn of the future Nation."[29]

The concept of seven-generation stewardship urges us to live and work for the benefit of the seventh generation into the future.[30]

Now that we know the secrets of nuclear fission and nuclear fusion; chemical and biological warfare; and radioactive Plutonium-239 with a half-life of 24,000 years, we have no choice but to think in terms of seven-generation stewardship.

EXPANDING 1928 MASTER PLANS

Expanding the city master plan from five to nine aspects will require a city to adopt a new way of looking at planning.

The City Planning Primer of 1928 was written just before it become clear that there was more to city planning than the placement of streets, buildings, and parks. It was written a year before parks became Hoovervilles where the dispossessed could set up shelters out of the weather. We now know that people need much more. They need to have the feeling of social well-being. But the planning profession has been slow to change; planners have had difficulty accepting this paradigm shift.

The new approach and underlying assumptions will have to come from someplace other than traditional city planning. In my search for a template to follow, I first looked at templates that states require their cities to follow. None of them led me to exactly what I needed, but California came close to providing me with what I was looking for.

California specific plans. California has expanded its general plans to include "specific plans," plans that focus on the neighborhood and development of small land areas. Specific plans, because they are much more detailed, have a better chance of creating a sense of place and attachment than do general plans.

California's specific plan pointed me in the right direction, but I still needed more flexibility.[31] Eventually I stumbled upon the Small Business Administration's business plan guidelines. A business plan turned out to be the template I was seeking.

A business-like approach. According to the U.S. Small business

Administration, a "business plan is an essential roadmap for business success."[32] The Small Business Administration recommends a business plan guideline that meets the needs of both business and government. They both need plans that center on sustainability.

Some may argue that the Small Business Administration might not be the best authority to cite when discussing land-use planning, but I don't agree. The SBA has the most experience with successful plans. Most city and regional plans fail because they lack the hard-nosed pragmatism required of business plans. For a land-use plan to be successful, it must be every bit as pragmatic as a business plan. Cities, like businesses, need to be profitable. Otherwise, they are operating as Ponzi schemes, living off of planning permit fees earned by approving ever more sprawl.

Failure to thrive. The marketplace is unforgiving. A business that fails to make a profit ends up bankrupt. A few examples:

- Blockbuster video rentals (1985–2010)
- Borders bookstores (1971–2011)
- General Motors (1908–2009)

In 2018 alone, there were 22,232 business failures in the United States.[33] Similarly, a city that fails to provide adequate sustenance, the necessities of life, ends up as a ghost town. There are more than 3,800 ghost towns in the U.S.[34]

THE INTRINSIC GOAL

The intrinsic goal of both businesses and cities has always been survival—the continuation of existence.

Before sustainability became trendy, it was said that the goal of every business was to generate as much profit as possible, and the goal of every city was to supply the necessities of life—food, shelter, medical attention, and protection from harm. Profits and the necessities of life still drive day-to-day management. But looking into the future, seven-generation sustainability must come to dominate long-range planning.

City-building professions. Cities come into being through the interaction of many trades and professions. Each of the three-principal city-building professions have a role to play:

- Architects provide framework—they build a sense of place.
- Engineers solve problems—they build a wall to hold back the flood.
- Planners avoid problems—they build the city on higher ground.

These three professions need to work together, but they must also provide checks and balances for one another. All three can be prone to short-term thinking, but they need to think in terms of seven-generation sustainability.

THE LOCAL PLANNING PROCESS

The local planning process requires continual research—collecting worldwide, regional, and local information. Few businesses or cities conduct sufficient research, because they simply don't realize how important it can be. These are a few simple ways to stay informed:

Newspaper clipping service. One research tool used by those in the know is the media monitoring service, or clipping service. Monitoring provides clients with media content of specific interest to them. Monitoring services offer coverage by subject, industry, size, geography, publication, etc. Spies use it—and you should, too. According to Universal-Information Services "as much as 70% of published news is not freely available online."[35]

Historical tabulation. Another research approach requires keeping track of historical events that have brought calamity to the community. I remember when I was a child and a neighbor pointed out to my father the high-water line of debris left behind when the river had flooded more than 80 years before. That prompted my father to build our new home 200 feet further up the hill. A few years later, the hundred-year flood washed away our old cabin, the county road, and the 80-year-old covered bridge crossing the river. If we hadn't been warned, we would have been washed away just as so many of our neighbors were. That's why many governments now record and list rare occurrences: they don't want to be taken by surprise when the rare event comes again.

Researching breakthroughs. The media is filled with stories about new energy sources, autonomous vehicles, construction innovations, alternative housing, and workplace innovation. Some of the new technology will transform city life, and cities need to be prepared. One company, GreenBiz Research, says that it "explores critical topics . . . to assess trends and market opportunities."[36]

Researching dead horses. Many public works projects are dead horses. Light rail and transit buses will be no match for autonomous vehicles that can pick up and deliver passengers from door to door. And social welfare programs are no substitute for jobs that pay living wages. New technologies are continually replacing older technologies—it's just how society works.

THE FOUR LEVELS OF PLANNING

Any business plan or governmental plan should address more than just getting up and running—it should also address layers of complexity such as target customers, customer needs, direct and indirect competitors, competitive advantages, pricing, and promotions to attract new customers.

Over time the business plan has undergone many iterations, until it has evolved into four descending levels. Cities should also write four level plans, plans that address many of the same issues as business plans.

HIERARCHY OF PLANS		
Status	**Business**	**Government**
Level 1	Strategic	General
Level 2	Tactical	Limited
Level 3	Operational	Specific
Level 4	Contingency	Emergency

RULES OF THE ROAD

Most states require their cities to adopt general plans and to periodically review and revise their local plans—though I don't know of any state that requires seven-generation planning.

Annual review. An annual review is essential to good planning. Without it, local plans lose their vitality.

Planning horizon. A plan is usually intended to look out into the future and present goals that will govern what's done for the next 20 years. City planners generally suggest that a plan be reviewed annually and substantially revised every five years.

Optimal length. The Small Business Administration suggests, "[A] business plan can range in size from 38 to 50 pages for a basic plan to as high as 80 to 100 pages for complex plans."[37] From my own experience writing plans, I would say that the page count should be about the same for local plans. If a plan is more than 100 pages long, very few people will read it. Let's face it—long plans are boring.

THE LITERACY QUAGMIRE

Literacy is defined as the ability to read and write—in order to function in society, to achieve personal goals, and to develop knowledge. The National Institute for Literacy estimates that 32 million American adults are unable to read.[38]

Functional illiteracy. A functional illiterate is a person who has had some schooling but does not meet a minimum standard of literacy. The Organization for Economic Cooperation and Development found that 50 percent of U.S. adults can't read a book written at an eighth-grade level. [39]

These 32 million functionally illiterate people are not going to be reading your local plans—and they are probably going to be completely left out of the planning process.

Writing in plain language. "Plain language" is a movement that started by simplifying unintelligible legal documents, and it has now been embraced by governments and businesses around the world. Plain language is clear, concise, and easily understood the first time someone reads or hears it. A plan must be written in plain language if it is be of value.[40]

According to Natalie Wexler, chair of the board of trustees for the Writing Revolution, "It's no secret that many Americans are lousy writers. Just ask any college professor or employer, including those at prestigious institutions. . . . In 2011, a nationwide test found that only 24 percent of students in eighth and 12th grades were proficient in writing."[41]

American writing has deteriorated to the point where the federal government had to adopt the Plain Writing Act of 2010, requiring that federal agencies use clear government communication that the public can understand and use.[42]

Write for your audience—likely to be readers at the eighth-grade level.

WORLD POPULATION IN 2100

"The goal of planning is to guide the development of a city or town so that it furthers the welfare of its current and future residents by creating convenient, equitable, healthful, efficient and attractive environments."[43] You can't write a plan without knowing the present population and the future population—local plans are population based.

According to the Pew Research Center, based on information collected by the United Nations, the world's population will stop increasing by the year 2100.[44]

By the year 2100, the world's population will stabilize at about 10.9 billion, with annual growth of less than 0.1 percent. A growth rate of only 0.1 percent, I would say, is virtually zero population growth—the point where the birth rate equals the death rate.

1. By the year 2100, the fertility rate is expected to be 1.9 births per woman—below the replacement fertility rate of 2.1 births per woman.
2. By 2100, both Europe and Latin America will have declining populations. Europe's population will peak at 748 million.
3. The United States and Canada will continue to grow in population due to migration from the rest of the world right up to the year 2100.
4. The population of Asia will increase from 4.6 billion in 2020 to 5.3 billion in 2055, then start to decline. China's population will peak in 2031, while the populations of Japan and South Korea will decline after 2020. India's population will grow until 2059, when it will reach 1.7 billion. Indonesia, the most populous country in Southeastern Asia, will reach its peak population in 2067.
5. Ninety countries are expected to lose population between 2020 and 2100 —including 32 out of the 48 countries in Europe.

6. By 2100, half of the 50 nations, territories and dependencies of Latin America and the Caribbean will lose population.

7. Between 2020 and 2100, Africa's population will increase from 1.3 billion to 4.3 billion. Africa will be the only region with strong population growth. But Africa is a special case. According to Sabine Balk of D+C Development and Cooperation, a website that discusses international-development affairs and explores how they relate to other fields of policy-making, reports that in a study by the German Institute for International and Security Affairs, "[the] authors argue that the sustained desire to have many children partly results from governments having done nothing to curb population growth in many countries or even fostering it in some places.[45] If outside social service agencies were to intervene, the African population could be much lower by the year 2100.

USA POPULATION IN 2100

As of 2020, the United States had a population of about 331 million. By the year 2062, the country will reach a maximum population of about 364 million. After that the population will decline to about 336 million by the year 2100, according to Richard Horton, editor of the British medical journal *The Lancet*.[46] The fertility rate in the U.S.—the average number of children a woman delivers over her lifetime—will steadily decline from 1.8 in 2017 to 1.5 in 2100. That's below the 2.1 birth rate required to maintain the existing population level without immigration.[47]

What the demographics show is that the United States has already nearly reached zero population growth. Soon it must decide whether to take in more people from around the world to keep its population growing or to reduce immigration to stabilize the population. And then the country must decide whether to live bunched up in a few megacities or to live in many small cities spread out across the continent.

The era of out-of-control population growth is behind us. Now the nations of the world will be given an opportunity to stop growing more crowded and start growing wiser, keeping the common good in mind.

Chapter 2
THE GENERAL PLAN

Traditionally, city planners refer to the overall 20 year first-level plan as the "general plan" or the "comprehensive plan." The general plan is very much like the strategic plan a business would write in order to answer these eight questions:

What is the economic trend?

What is the type of business?

What is of value to the customer?

Which services should be offered?

Which services should be excluded?

What is the geographic scope?

What is the competitive advantage?

What is the occupational outlook advantage?[41]

1. WHAT IS THE ECONOMIC TREND?

The economic trend is an indicator that shows how the local economy is doing. The growth path of a city is nearly identical to that of a business: development; start-up; growth; expansion; and maturity.

My own experience with growth. I started delivering newspapers when I was a middle school student. My 60-customer route sprawled across a quarter of the city where I lived. Over a short period of time, I added more than 60 new customers to my route—but the newspaper company said that 120 newspapers were too many for a middle school student to deliver. They took away half of my route. That taught me not to take on so many new customers so quickly. So, I sold off inconvenient outlying blocks of customers to other newspaper boys. Then I found out how to buy newspapers wholesale directly from the press room and sell them without the district manager finding out about it. Soon I built my route up to 120 customers again—but because I had sold my time-wasting fringe-area customers, I could deliver all 120 newspapers in 15 minutes. After that, the newspaper management left me alone and I got to make some real money—$336 a month in today's inflated dollars. Not bad for a 13-year-old!

Growth—right-sizing. Cities should think the same way as a newspaper boy might—is it better to grow bigger or to grow smaller? As reported in the Memphis Commercial Appeal:

"The city of Memphis will trim a roughly two-square-mile section of South Cordova from its boundaries over the next two years, giving residents of the area a victory in a fight they've waged for years.

"With this de-annexation, the third and last in a planned series aimed at decreasing the strain on city services extending to Memphis' sprawling outer reaches, the city will shed roughly 4,000 residents and about 1,800 housing units spread across 2.3 square miles.

"Councilman J. Ford Canale said the move will allow the city to reinvest in some of its core neighborhoods, and characterized it as "right-sizing" the city."[48]

Economies of scale. according to Investopedia, "Economies of scale are cost advantages [achieved by] increasing production and lowering costs. This happens because costs are spread over a larger number of goods." But, economies of scale often have limits, such as passing the point where costs per additional unit begin to increase.

In regard to cities, there is no solid evidence to support the claim that big cities are more cost efficient than small towns. Eventually bigger cities run up against diseconomies of scale—disadvantages that increase due to the per-unit costs of providing services. These are some examples from California:

The city of Half Moon Bay denied a subdivision permit because the proposal would add 100 homes, requiring the city to build a multimillion-dollar sewage plant.

The city of Mountain View stopped construction of a 12-story office building after learning that it would have to spend millions of dollars on fire-fighting equipment that it couldn't afford.

As reported in the 2002 California Planning & Development Report, "Caltrans completed the Highway 101 freeway from the Golden Gate Bridge into Sonoma County [in 1969]. The freeway transformed Petaluma into the northernmost bedroom community for workers in San Francisco. In 1970, builders erected about 600 homes in Petaluma, [and] 900 in 1971. The rapid growth overwhelmed public services: Schools went to double sessions and the wastewater treatment system failed. In 1972, Petaluma voters capped approval of new homes at 500 units per year."[49]

The NewGeography study. Urban policy analyst Wendell Cox, writing in NewGeography Magazine tells us that "local government consolidation and regional governance is all the rage in policy circles"[50] but there is no evidence that consolidation creates an economy of scale. The NewGeography study found that Pennsylvania's largest jurisdictions spent 150 percent more per capita and New York's largest jurisdictions spent nearly 200 percent more per capita than jurisdictions of 5,000 to 10,000 population.

The NewGeography study also found that "America's small-town government structure engenders a sense of community, even as a part of larger metropolitan areas. They also save a lot of money because democracy works better when government is closer to home."[51] The study concluded, "It is not surprising that so many consolidation proposals fail and that when given the chance, voters usually reject consolidation proposals."[52]

Wendell Cox writes that "America is more 'small town' than we often think. In 2000, slightly more than one-half of the nation's population lived in jurisdictions with fewer than 25,000 people."[53] Cox goes on to say, "According to the 2002 U.S. Census of Governments, there were more than 34,000 local general-purpose governments with less than 25,000 residents . . . . With so many 'small towns,' the average population of [incorporated places] in the United States [is] 6,200."[54]

2. WHAT IS THE TYPE OF BUSINESS?

The answer is sometimes surprising, even to the business itself. As reported on the Wall Street Survivor website, "Former McDonald's CFO, Harry J. Sonneborn, is even quoted as saying, 'we are not technically in the food business. We are in the real estate business. The only reason we sell fifteen-cent hamburgers is because they are the greatest producer of revenue, from which our tenants can pay us our rent.'"[55]

In regard to city planning, Mark Funkhouser, former publisher of Governing magazine and former mayor of Kansas City: "Government in a democracy is essentially a conservative institution. It is responsible for creating and sustaining markets, enforcing contracts, protecting private property, and producing systems of education and infrastructure that allow commerce to function efficiently."[56]

A city needs to govern, not pretend to be all things to all people—many cities have run up long range debt that will be extremely hard to pay off. The internet lists these debtor cities where investors, relocation agents, and families on the move can see them, and avoid them.

3. WHAT IS OF VALUE TO THE CUSTOMER?

There are numerous websites that list the worst places to live in America, and the results vary widely. But the top reasons that people are moving away from these places seem to be safety issues.

Maslow's personal security needs. In his book *A Theory of Human Motivation*, Abraham Maslow lists these as being among basic human needs: personal security (absence of physical threat); financial security (absence of financial hardship); health and well-being (absence of illness or infirmity); and a safety net against accidents and illness, and their adverse impacts (ability to receive appropriate medical care). A city that can't adequately provide for these needs will soon find itself on the skids:

High crime rate—physical threat. People need to feel personally secure.

No jobs—financial hardship. People move to where the jobs are. We've been doing this for some 315 thousand years, since the inception of Homo sapiens.[57]

Unhealthy surroundings—illness or infirmity. People move away from smog, trash, abandoned buildings, and concrete jungles.

No local hospital—appropriate medical care. "At least 30 hospitals entered bankruptcy in 2019, according to data compiled by Bloomberg. They range from Hahnemann University Hospital in downtown Philadelphia to De Queen Medical Center in rural Sevier County, Arkansas."[58]

4. WHICH SERVICES SHOULD BE OFFERED?

Cities typically provide streets, public libraries, water, sewage, drainage, garbage, fire protection, paramedics, and police services. Some cities also provide public schools, food inspection and other public services, and public transit. Cities may also operate or contract for electricity, gas, and cable television. Cities with better-educated populations typically offer more cultural services, such as museums, zoos, aquariums, and performance venues.

5. WHICH SERVICES SHOULD BE EXCLUDED?

If you went to your city council and asked them to build a church for your congregation, you would probably be reminded of what Thomas Jefferson called the "wall of separation between church and state." Mixing state and church affairs is an inherently bad idea. But so is becoming a lender of last resort.

Lordstown GM plant. In 2009, Ohio, offered General Motors massive tax breaks to help it expand and retool its Lordstown plant. Under the terms of the deal, GM got a 75 percent income tax reduction for 15 years, worth $14.2 million, for agreeing to add 200 new jobs at the plant until 2039.

In a separate agreement, Ohio gave General Motors an additional $46.1 million in tax breaks if it kept the number of existing employees at 3,700 until 2027. Then, in 2018, General Motors announced that it would end production on March, 2019.

In 2020, the state of Ohio told General Motors that it would have to repay more than $60 million in public subsidies because it closed the Lordstown plant before 2027.

According to Greg LeRoy, executive director of Good Jobs First, a national nonprofit that advocates for accountability in economic development. "If the state were to claw back $60 million, that would be one of the biggest claw back events in U.S. history."[59]

Officials were outraged. U.S. Sen. Sherrod Brown, D-Ohio, said that GM's decision was "corporate greed at its worst."[60] But it was not. It was a matter of a state government making a financial decision based on magical thinking rather than on economic analysis—bad governance. Cities should never bailout private companies, that is a task best left for banks and investors to perform.

Oakland Raiders. Cities often shy away from providing commercial leisure-time venues such as golf courses and amusement parks, but the same does not seem to apply to professional sport stadiums. As Rick Paulas wrote in *The Atlantic* in 2018:

". . . whereas nearly every other business funds the construction of its facilities and pays taxes too, cities often give money to private pro-sports franchises to entice them to come, and then give them even more to stay.

"The Coliseum . . . lured the Raiders back to Oakland in 1994 in part by promising to renovate. When that bill is finally paid off in 2025, it will have cost Alameda County and Oakland $350 million. It seems worth pointing out that the Raiders' value has skyrocketed from $351 million in 2001 to $2.38 billion in 2017. . . . Meanwhile, Oakland's roads are some of the worst in the country, the Oakland Unified School District is cutting up to 340 jobs for the 2019–20 school year, and the city has to rely on outside spending to cover the mostly inadequate shelter it provides its homeless population. . . ." [Note that as of this year the Raiders have moved to Las Vegas.]

Super Bowl tailgate party. Imagine a stadium as a giant drain.

Money flows from the community into the stadium, where it whirls around for a bit, then funnels down some murky pipes to exit far, far away. Some leaves with the players, some with owners and ownership groups, some with the league itself, the headquarters of which are in New York. That last leakage is similar to what happens when you shop at a corporate chain. . . . Worse, the new activity may actually hurt the overall economy by "crowding out" other events.

"In 2016, when San Francisco hosted the Super Bowl, the city paid to reroute cars and buses, to fund police overtime for security, and for sanitation workers clean it all up. In all, the city spent an estimated $9.6 million. . . . 'Restaurants were telling us they had a 40 to 50 percent reduction in reservations and services,' says San Francisco Supervisor Jane Kim, who was outspoken against this deal at the time. 'I don't think public taxpayers should subsidize a party for a $12.4 billion company.'"[61]

Sports teams are businesses not pets. They, like other businesses should obtain funding from investors and banks, not government.

6. WHAT IS THE GEOGRAPHIC SCOPE?

A city's geographic scope is its incorporation boundary. Some cities craft their boundaries to maximize benefits and minimize costs. Others annex all the land they can, because they just want to be big. I live adjacent to two Arizona cities, Peoria and Glendale, both of which are urban sprawl offering nothing at all. They seem to exist only to annex more and more raw land.

Peoria appears to be so greedy for land that it is annexing whatever it can in two counties, Maricopa and Yavapai. What's next—annexing Utah?

7.WHAT IS THE COMPETITIVE ADVANTAGE?

According to Ovidijus Jurevicius, writing for *Strategic Management Insight*, "If a company can't identify one [competitive advantage] or just doesn't possess it, competitors soon outperform it and force the business to leave the market. There are many ways to achieve the advantage but only two basic types of it: cost or differentiation advantage."[62]

If your city has a competitive advantage, you know what it is. If not, you are going to have to create one from scratch. Says Steve Olenski in *Forbes* magazine, "In recent years, cities have realized the value of creating a brand image to attract businesses, residents, and tourists. Creating a successful city brand is much like creating a product or personal brand. You've got to go through a discovery stage to determine what your city can offer. If you find you don't have some of the elements needed to attract your desired audience, devise a plan to develop them."[63]

First impressions. Driving to your city on the freeway, the investor with the money sees your landscaping or lack thereof; your boulevards separating cars from homes, or the miles of strip commercial with flashing-blinking-animated signs; your free-flowing river and shoreline park, or the concrete channel with chain-link fencing.

Every city should understand that the investor looking for an opportunity isn't going to be fooled by smoke and mirrors. If you don't know what I mean, watch the action-comedy film *The Interview*—the movie in which the protagonists find that North Korean merchandise displays are just painted on the store windows.[64] It's a funny movie.

Theming. There are plenty of ways to spruce up your city. One of them is theming. I did all my redevelopment work in a city that was home to Juan Bautista Valentín Alvarado y Vallejo, who was governor of Las Californias from 1837 to 1842. The city's redevelopment agency themed the city to incorporate early California history, creating a sense of place.

Branding. Another way to enhance a city's appeal is by branding. "I ♥ NY" is one example. Your city needs to stand out from the competition.

"Today, the Mile-High City [Denver] may have a secondary meaning beyond its height above sea level. It's now a leader in cannabis. While this may seem like a risky way to position a city brand, it's worked, primarily due to the shift in legislation and perspective regarding cannabis."[65]

And don't overlook these tongue-in-cheek brands:
- And on the sixth day, God created MANchester.
- Canberra: Sex, Lies, and Red Tape.
- Welcome to Oregon—now go home.

8. WHAT IS THE OCCUPATIONAL OUTLOOK?

Since 1948, the United States Department of Labor's Bureau of Labor Statistics has compiled information about occupations in this country:
- The *Occupational Outlook Handbook* provides information about the nature of various types of work, working conditions, education, earnings, and job outlook for hundreds of different occupations.[66]
- The *Career Guide to Industries* provides information about the nature of a particular business, working conditions, education, earnings, and job outlook for workers in dozens of different industries. This guide is no longer published by the

Bureau of Labor Statistics, but the information can now be found in other publications.[67]

Fastest-growing occupations. The world of work is changing fast. Many of the top occupations listed by the Bureau of Labor Statistics are of recent origin, and most are well-suited to women as well as men. Six of the fastest-growing jobs are in health care. Two top jobs—wind turbine technician and solar photovoltaic installer—are very physical. "Windtechs must . . . be capable of climbing ladder systems, often 260 feet high, [carrying] 45 pounds [of tools.]"[68] That would scare the bejesus out of me. Below is a list of fast-growing occupation. It changes slightly from year to year.

FASTEST-GROWING OCCUPATIONS 2018–2028[69]		
Occupation	**Growth Rate**	**Median Pay**
Solar photovoltaic installer	63	$42,680
Wind turbine service technician	57	$54,370
Home health aide	37	$24,200
Personal care aide	36	$24,020
Occupational therapy assistant	33	$60,220
Information security analyst	32	$98,350
Physician assistant	31	$108,610
Statistician	31	$87,780
Nurse practitioner	28	$107,030
Speech-language pathologist	27	$77,510

Fastest-shrinking occupations. Below are 15 jobs that are on their way out, according to Siôn Phillpott on the CareerAddict website. Furthermore, he writes, "A 2015 study by Foundation for Young Australians found that nearly 60% of young people in the country 'were studying or training for occupations where at least two-thirds of jobs will be automated' by the next decade or so. That is a huge waste of skills."[70]

FASTEST-SHRINKING OCCUPATIONS		
1. Travel agent	6. Textile worker	11. Lumberjack
2. Cashier	7. Printing press operator	12. Telemarketer
3. Fast food cook	8. Sports referee/Umpire	13. Fisher
4. Mail carrier	9. Retail jeweler	14. Legal secretary
5. Bank teller	10. Dispatcher	15. Assembler/Fabricator

The list should be no surprise to most of us—we've been trying to kill the umpire since the invention of baseball, but they've just kept multiplying: home plate umpire, first-base umpire, third-base umpire, left-field and right-field umpires. Most of the disappearing occupations won't be missed—only the paychecks.

Occupational outlook winners and losers. The San Francisco Bay Area and the Seattle area both specialize in high tech. Las Vegas specializes in separating you from your money. St. Louis, Missouri, specializes in crime—it's number one in the nation. But while St. Louis is being destroyed by crime, the Arizona town of Florence actually thrives on crime—other peoples' crime. Florence is home to multiple state, federal, county, and private prisons:

1. Arizona State Prison Complex – Florence
2. Arizona State Prison Complex – Eyman
3. Arizona State Prison Florence – West
4. Central Arizona Correctional Facility
5. Central Arizona Detention Center
6. Immigration and Customs Enforcement
7. Florence Correctional Center
8. The Pinal County Adult Detention Center
9. The Pinal County Youth Justice

Perhaps Pinal County should be renamed Penal County?

WHAT SHOULD THE CITY LOOK LIKE IN THE FUTURE?

The general plan envisions what a city should look like in the years to come. A well-crafted plan paints a picture of what the city should look like at full development and what it should look like at some intermediate point, usually 20 years in the future. I use the term "picture" because, in most cases, a city's general plan is a color-coded map showing future land uses. This may look simplistic, but to a professional city planner it provides a wealth of information in a snapshot, what would take reams of paper to express in words. Or, as they say, a picture is worth a thousand words.

In a city's general plan, most of the text elaborates on the land use map by explaining the reasoning behind the allocation of each color as a percentage and the pattern of the color-coded "mosaic" (such as 25 percent streets, 52 percent residential, 8 percent parks, and so on). The general plan also presents policies to ensure that the city will grow as shown on the land use map. The plan should be strong enough to control the way property development will take place over the long run while being flexible enough to accommodate unforeseen contingencies.

The general plan customarily applies to the entire area of the city and any land beyond its borders that may eventually be annexed. As a matter of practicality, a city needs a general plan that does all of the following:

- calculates the percentage of land needed for each type of land use
- establishes the path of growth
- estimates the rate of population growth

- schedules the installation date for new public utilities and services
- forestalls potential land use conflicts
- sets aesthetic standards as a component of land use governance

Right sizing. The general plan should define the city's maximum land area and maximum population. If it doesn't do so (and most plans don't), the city won't be able to effectively plan for the proper sizing of roads, pipes, wires, public buildings, or other utilities and facilities that must be designed for a defined population or land area. Failure to define population or land area parameters leads to endless rounds of premature infrastructure failure and expensive resizing—such as our unending expansion of urban freeways.

STATE PLANNING LAWS

- Each state has its own planning laws and general plan rules. I'm only going to explain the approaches used by the three most populous states: California, Texas, and Florida. America's three most populous states take three very different approaches toward their general plans:
- "Papa Bear" plans (California)—an over-concentration on the trivial
- "Momma Bear" plans (Florida)—a moderate approach: not too little, not too much
- "Baby Bear" plans (Texas)—as little planning as possible.

California: the "Papa Bear" approach. California requires each city and county to have a general plan with a 20-year horizon. The plan applies to all territory within the city limits and any "land outside its boundaries, which in the planning agency's judgment bears relation to its planning."[71] The general plan is intended to present a clear set of guideposts for achieving the jurisdiction's long-term physical development goal. California Government Code (Section 65302) lists seven elements that must be addressed:

- **Land Use.** Proposes the general distribution of land for housing, business, industry, etc. It also states the anticipated number of inhabitants, dwellings, and other land uses per acre.
- **Circulation.** Describes the general location of major thoroughfares, transportation routes, terminals, etc.
- **Housing.** Not related to any other general plan element, this is specific rather than general, narrow rather than comprehensive, and short-range rather than long-range. It is usually presented as a separate, stand-alone document.
- **Conservation.** Addresses development and use of natural resources, including water.
- **Open Space.** Provides for preservation of natural resources, including plants and animals. This duplicates much of which is in the conservation element.
- **Noise.** Measures "sound volume" but not, in fact, noise. "Sound" is the surf crashing against your boathouse, the hum of urban living, the sounds from streets, freeways, airports, and the like; "noise" is your neighbor's teenager blasting a boom box when you're trying to get some sleep.
- **Safety.** Protects the community from earthquakes, floods, fires, and other disasters, natural and human-caused.

Florida: the "Momma Bear" approach. Florida cities and counties must adopt general or comprehensive plans that address the following elements:

- **Future Land Use.** This plans for the amount and type of land use needed for future population growth.
- **Housing.** Explains how all economic groups will be provided housing. It also addresses substandard dwelling replacement.

- **Traffic Circulation.** Plans for the types, locations, and sizes of major roads that will be needed to accommodate traffic growth.
- **Recreation and Open Space.** Plans for natural and built recreation and open space.
- **Capital Improvements.** Schedules public facility funding and construction for at least the following five years.
- **Intergovernmental Coordination.** Explains how the jurisdiction will coordinate its planning with other jurisdictions.
- **Infrastructure.** Explains how potable water, storm water, sanitary sewer waste, solid waste, and groundwater aquifer recharge will be managed for at least the next 10 years.
- **Conservation.** Plans for the conservation of natural resources, including air, water, water recharge, and wetlands.
- **Public-School Facilities.** Plans for adequate K–12 schools to meet future residential growth.
- **Coastal management.** Coastal cities and counties must have an element that protects human life from hurricanes and other natural disasters and addresses coastal environmental quality.
- **Optional elements.** A comprehensive plan may include elements such as economic development, historic preservation, or community design.
- **Future land use.** A Florida comprehensive plan must include a map that shows the location and extent of future development.

Texas: the "Baby Bear" approach. Texas doesn't require local governments to plan. The general or comprehensive plan, if a local government chooses to adopt one, must present land use policies based on the analysis of existing physical, economic, and social conditions; it guides public decision-making regarding land use, capital improvements, and other land management decisions. A comprehensive plan map (if there is one) must also contain a clearly visible statement that says, "A comprehensive plan shall not constitute zoning regulations or establish zoning district boundaries."

Many Texans are adamantly opposed to zoning, so some city halls get around this attitude by disguising zoning regulations as other kinds of legal provisions. This ruse usually works. But Hurricane Harvey flooded Houston in 2017 because all those Texans who oppose planning and zoning in principle didn't bother to plan for such an event. Now they want the rest of America to bail them out— thank y'all.

No outstanding differences. Drive across America and you won't see any outstanding differences in the look of urbanization between states with Papa Bear, Momma Bear, or Baby Bear planning laws. In actuality, the quality of urban development is controlled by real-estate developers, not planners. Much of the time, government planning is just busywork. Maybe American city planning took a wrong turn somewhere along the way. Why do so many of us find ourselves living in cardboard cities that leave us longing for home?

NINE DEVELOPMENT ASPECTS

A city's general plan needs to address nine development aspects in enough detail to give direction to real estate developers, the people who bring cities into being by turning raw land into urban places. The general plan needs to explain what the residents of the city want and what they don't want. In a way, the general plan is a sales pitch aimed at attracting real estate developers who share values with the people who live in the city. If the general plan is successful, new real estate development and redevelopment will seamlessly blend into the existing urban fabric.

1. ECONOMIC TREND CITY WIDE

The general plan is concerned with residential, commercial, and industrial economic trends, and the most desirable path of growth for various land uses.

Measuring the land. The first task in writing a general plan is to accurately measure the land area—preferably by using the time-tested methodology perfected in the 1930s by one of America's premier city planners, Harland Bartholomew, who conducted land use studies involving 97 cities and urban areas across America.[72] Bartholomew devised a system for comparing the extent and intensity of urban land use, starting with a city's legal boundaries as the basic land area to be analyzed. From this he subtracted the raw land; that is to say, he excluded all the land that wasn't part of the built-up city. This compensated for the fact that many cities extend their legal boundaries well out into the countryside in expectation of future growth. By excluding exurban and agricultural land, Bartholomew achieved a true picture of urban land use intensity.

When Bartholomew examined land use data from central cities, he found that in general only about 56 percent of a city's land was developed for some sort of urban use. He also found that larger cities have a higher population density than smaller cities. Follow-up studies confirm that this happens whether or not a city has a master plan or an urban general plan.

There is very little chance that the city you live in will have the same land use distribution by percentage as the cities inventoried by Bartholomew. Land use has changed since he conducted his studies back in the 1930s; for example, we now have more land used for automobiles and less for railroads. What I want you to understand is that there are constraints on how land can be distributed in a city, and there are discernible patterns. You won't find a city with 80 percent street right-of-way—such a city would be little more than traffic—but you could find a city with 80 percent commercial use. And while the Las Vegas Strip has thirty-eight casinos on a four-mile strip of land, that's probably a few more than you have in your town.[73] Some cities try to eliminate industrial land, such as Atherton, California, an icon of wealth and luxury; others, such as the City of Industry in California, are—as its name proclaims—nearly all industrial.

Street right of way. A land inventory can start with any element of land use. I like to start with street right-of-way—the land reserved for streets—because the less land you use for streets, the better for the city. As a rule, streets don't pay property taxes, streets are made (figuratively speaking) of oil, and streets are maintained at public expense. A city that is thrifty with street right-of-way leaves more land for other uses, especially uses that contribute property taxes.

Streets account for the second largest use of urban land. About 28 percent of developed land is paved for streets. Early twenty-first-century suburban cities probably use quite a bit more than that average, but sophisticated planning techniques can cut street right-of-way down to as little as 18 percent of developed land.

A few years ago, Minnesota-based Rick Harrison Site Design came up with a concept called "coving"—"an alternative to traditional grid-style planning that focuses on siting homes on nonuniform lot shapes along curved streets. The goal is a minimum of pavement and a maximum of green space." It's worth looking at (http://www.rhsd-planning.com/).

Residential land distribution. Harland Bartholomew found that, on average, more land is used for residences than for any other use—about 40 percent. However, every community is different. Some cities keep industries out, while others try to become industrial centers.

Commercial land distribution. If you take a close look at a group of cities, you will most likely find a growing number of nearly empty older shopping centers. Many shopping centers in and around America's old downtowns have emptied out following the building of big-box retail outlets on the edges of towns. In addition, internet purchases have taken away some of the old shopping centers' business.

Overexpansion of commercial land has led to a nationwide oversupply of shopping centers. Trying to force more land into commercial use than a city actually needs can easily lead to oversupply, low rents, bankruptcies, and vacant stores—and that's exactly what is happening. I've seen plans that set aside as much as 25 percent of a city's total land area for commerce. Realistically, cities use only somewhere from 3 to 7 percent of land for commerce.

As for online shopping: surveys find that shoppers tend to buy small appliances, books, and bulky items online and purchase clothing and groceries at their local shopping centers. Brick-and-mortar stores aren't going away, but they will have to adjust to the new competition.

Industrial and railroad land. The cities studied by Bartholomew in the 1930s used around 12 percent of their land for railroads and industry. He also found that major industrial areas, once spread along railroad routes, were even then moving away from railroads toward highways and airports.

Today many industrial properties are plagued by obsolete public infrastructure. To bring industrial land into the twenty-first century, your city may need to stop thinking in terms of "light industrial" and "heavy industrial"—two increasingly obsolete designations. Instead, consider substituting the concept of "intrusive" and "unintrusive" industrial land use. Intrusive industries are industries that produce odor, noise, and heavy rail or truck traffic, and have generally unpleasant aesthetics. Most twenty-first-century industries are unintrusive— software development, for example, or app designs for your smart phone, computer code writing, and all that other stuff they did on the TV series *Halt and Catch Fire*. They are so clean and quiet that they can easily blend in with adjacent residential neighborhoods.

One San Francisco Bay Area city where "starter homes" sell for around $2 million allowed an industrial park to be built in a residential neighborhood adjacent to a neighborhood shopping center. The lavishly landscaped "unintrusive industrial" park blends in seamlessly with the surrounding multimillion-dollar housing. The microscopic-size products produced here are based on recent advances in computing, biotech, and robotics and are shipped out daily by USPS, FedEx, or UPS. The doctoral-level researchers walk to work. Most neighboring residents think the buildings house medical and dental offices.

Vacant land. A city's raw feedstock is land. When a city runs out of land, it either stops growing or increases its density by growing vertically. General plans usually ignore reserve land, assuming it is not really a class of land use. But vacant land is every bit as important as any other land, and it serves a function in city building. Bartholomew found in the 1930s that about one-third of the land in small cities was left vacant or not used for urban purposes. Even in densely populated urban areas, some land always remains vacant or underused. This adds up to a lot of potential infill construction opportunity.

Even the most crowded cities have vacant land where new buildings could be constructed if zoning regulations were more flexible. In Palm Springs, California, where we used to live, many "remainder" lots too small to be developed in compliance with city zoning could be developed as "small homes" that are below the city's minimum square footage. Not every home needs to have a 120-foot frontage, especially now that 27.5 percent of Americans live alone.[74]

Parks and open space. Harland Bartholomew found that parks and playgrounds averaged less than 7 percent of developed land. Parkland is some of the most valuable land a city can have, but many cities so undervalue it that they allow most of their parks to be sited on "remainders"—land left over after subdivisions have been built. Remainder land is cheap, but rarely in the right spot for a park. The Planning Advisory Service report "Standards for Outdoor Recreational Areas"[75] presents standards for many types of parks, including playgrounds, neighborhood parks, community parks, and major parks.

Charles Downing Lay was a landscape architect for the New York State Department of Parks in the early twentieth century.[76] In 1914 he recommended that 12.5 percent of city land be used as parkland.[77] Since then, the percentage of recreational land per capita in the largest cities has increased, while parkland in surrounding suburbs has decreased. American suburbs need *more* parkland, not less.

Mismeasuring land. Before anyone writes a general plan, the city's land has to be accurately measured. If it isn't, the plan writers will reach erroneous conclusions, and the plan will lead decision-makers astray. Some plans mistakenly lump urban and rural land together before calculating the total area available for urbanization. Rural land must be kept separate until it is officially opened up for urban development. Some plans list membership golf courses, locked schoolyards, and vacant private land as parkland. Unless the land can be used by the general public for recreation, it should not be counted as parkland.

The correct way to measure the width of a street is to copy the measurement from the official plat kept on file in the county recorder's office. The wrong way is to go out in the field and measure the pavement width. The pavement width is always much narrower than the legal street right-of-way. The discrepancy will be at least ten feet, maybe a lot more. The plat is always more dependable. If plan writers mismeasure the land, the plan will mislead all the people who have to rely on the accuracy of that measurement. That could end up costing city hall a lot more than it had bargained for.

The thing to notice in Bartholomew's methodology is the amount of land used for street rights-of-way. Cities derive their base income from property taxes; streets are not taxed. On the other hand, commercial and industrial land generates tax revenue and provides jobs and the "necessaries" of life.

Since I went to planning school half a century ago, the art of measuring land has been lost. Nowadays, planners sometimes feel obligated to pretend to measure the land, but they don't know how to do it, or why it is important. The following table is from a small city I worked for back in the early 1970s. It shows how far planners have drifted away from applying the knowledge base created by the master—Harland Bartholomew.

THE NEW LAND MISMEASUREMENT METHODOLOGY LAND USE DISTRIBUTION IN ACRES, 2011		
	Total Land at Buildout	**Percent of Land at Buildout**
Low Density Residential	526.51	41
Medium Density Residential	170.5	13
High Density Residential	66.4	05
Mixed Use Center North	2.7	01
Mixed Used Center South	16.1	01
Commercial Mixed Use	57.3	04
Residential Mixed Use	13.9	01
Neighborhood Commercial	41.1	03
Regional Commercial	58.3	05
Entertainment District	22.1	02

Industrial Mixed Use	26.4	02
Public Institutional	231.6	18
Parks and Open Space	57.3	04
Total Land Area	1290.2	100

Whoever devised this table thought it added up to 100 percent—but it doesn't. *They forgot to measure the street right-of-way!* When I measured the same city in 1974, I found that streets used 18.5 percent of the land—a small amount. Some sprawling cities use as much as 35 percent of the city's land for their streets. What happens when it comes time to repave? Who is going to pay for all that excess pavement?

The path of growth. A city should move away from prime farmland, conservation land, and flood plains. But most cities do just the opposite.

Arizona's Phoenix Metropolitan Area, made up of a group of sprawling cities, had to choose between moving east toward higher ground that cost more to develop or moving west toward prime farmland, the Palo Verde Nuclear Generating Station, and Luke Air Force Base. The local leaders chose to move both east, toward higher ground and west, toward radioactivity and deafening noise. In January 2019, "for the first time, there were more than 1,000 F-35 flights from the base in one month . . . . Surprise city councilman Chris Judd said he hasn't noticed an increase in flights lately. He said noise from the flights is 'just part of living' in his district."[78]

The way the wind blows. About all you might need to know about the path of growth is which way the wind blows.

In Fresno, California, the general plan set aside the south end of the city for heavy industrial land use. Over the years this vicinity attracted a mountain of garbage, a sewage works, chicken processing, cattle slaughtering, lard processing, and other aromatic land uses. But when subprime lending came along in 2003, the city couldn't resist helping out its "friends" by rezoning a parcel of vacant land in the heavy industrial area so that low-end single-family homes could be built on the farmland south of those aromatic land uses.

The new homes were sold in the winter, when the winds blew from the south. But as the weather heated up and the winds shifted to their prevailing direction—north to south—the homebuyers found out why their homes had been so inexpensive. Nearly all of these families had financed their purchases with no-money-down subprime mortgages. But they had no idea they'd bought stinkers. When the wind shifted, some sued, but most just moved away from what had becoming "upside down" homes that quickly lost value.

When I investigated the situation, I drove over to the garbage mountain that had by then been covered by a thin layer of dirt and renamed Hyde Park. One of the families I talked to walked up the mountain, and someone drove a pipe into the ground, took out a match, and set the pipe on fire. The kids thought this was great magic.

Now, of course, the heavy industries that had been built where nobody would care about the stench are blamed for the whole disaster—and blamed by the city that had issued the subdivision permit. Yet as *San Francisco Chronicle* writer Carl Nolte wrote, "There have always been two Fresnos: the one of [native son William] Saroyan and of admirers of the small-town feel of Fresno. The other was a town where the fix was always in. . . . But growth and the millions to be made from development introduced another dimension. Development could mean, as [Mark] Arax wrote, that 'a farmer barely meeting his mortgage could quadruple the value of his land by selling to the right developer with the political juice to finagle a rezoning.'"[79]

2. TRANSPORTATION CITY WIDE

A city's general plan is concerned with movement of all types to and from the locality and within the locality—major thoroughfares; street railways; bus lines, and other forms of rapid transit; railways, waterways, and harbor developments; and public utility plants, mains, conduits, and wires.

However, the biggest change in transportation is going to be the introduction of autonomous vehicles over the next 20 years—it will be a revolutionary change.

Airplanes and Hyperloop. I'm skipping over air travel and Hyperloop—the futuristic transportation method proposed by entrepreneur Elon Musk drawing on 100-year-old principals updated for the twenty-first century. You will have to do your own research on these two modes of travel. Hyperloop is about to be built somewhere, but just where has yet to be announced; it will be a revolutionary advancement.

Autonomous trucks. Autonomous trucks will eliminate many jobs and change the layout of streets, parking, and even the placement of buildings—and the change is already underway.

The Survival Tech Shop website says, "On average, a truck driver will go 55–60 miles per hour—that is, of course, if they adhere to federal, state, or interstate laws. Assuming that they drive for 11 hours, they average 600–650 miles per day. Of course, that number is open to fluctuation. There's a lot of variables: Weather, traffic, routes, and accidents all may alter the mileage."[80]

According to information from Truck Accident Attorney Network, critical driver error accounts for most crashes. "Accidents caused by this factor generally involves failure to adapt the speed to the road conditions, being unfamiliar with the road, fatigue, illegal maneuvers, distractions, OTC drug use, inadequate surveillance of the surroundings and nearby traffic, etc."[81]

If the truck driver you see driving along beside you looks like the straw-filled scarecrow from *The Wizard of Oz*, he is probably driving for TuSimple.

As reported by *Business Insider*, "TuSimple has partnered with companies like UPS and Penske Truck Leasing to create a network of autonomous freight delivery trucks across the US by 2024. . . . Phase one, which will take place between [2020] and 2021, will bring . . . trucking services to Phoenix and Tucson in Arizona, and El Paso, Dallas, Houston, and San Antonio in Texas, while phase two set between 2022 and 2023 will expand the network . . . from Los Angeles to Jacksonville, Florida."[82]

Autonomous vehicles are on the road, so the issue is no longer "will they work?" It is now a question of how soon we will all be riding around like that straw-filled scarecrow, in vehicles smarter than us?

How long does a conventional human driven, diesel powered, Class 8 truck (a large truck with an attached trailer that is used for hauling freight) last? Class 8 trucks have a 15-year cradle-to-grave life cycle, and cost about $118,000. The new Tesla electric Class 8 truck costs about $200,000—but the statistics are most impressive. Bart Simpson would give it a "holy cow!" Autonomous electric trucks are the future if they can drive themselves a consistent 500 miles a day. Right now, the Tesla has a range of 300 to 500 miles, just shy of the distance between terminals where they can recharge. Already, in the Phoenix Metropolitan Area, land prices are adjusting to accommodating the needs of autonomous trucks—freight transfer terminals are replacing restaurant and lodging truck stops. Autonomous trucks will run 24-7 needing only to refuel or recharge.

Autonomous ships. Port cities need to carefully prepare for a very different future. The first autonomous ship has already been built by Kongsberg Maritime of Norway. "The vessel YARA Birkeland will be the world's first fully electric and autonomous container ship, with zero emissions. . . . It will be a fully battery powered solution, prepared for autonomous and unmanned operation. . . .Loading and discharging will be done automatically using electric cranes and equipment. . . . The ship will also be equipped with an automatic mooring system—berthing and unberthing will be done without human intervention, and will not require special implementations dock-side. . . . Testing of autonomous capability will be carried out [in] 2020."[83]

The lifetime of a modern vessel is about 25 to 30 years.[84] Once the first autonomous ship is operational, why would anyone keep building obsolete crewed ships? So about 30 years from now you can expect the vast majority of ships to be autonomous and self-docking and self-loading. Not a lot of job creation, I'd say.[89]

Additionally, according to a study by Allianz, between 75 and 96 percent of maritime accidents are caused by human error. "There are also efficiencies realized in ship design and use of fuel. . . . [The] study projected savings of more than $7 million over 25 years per autonomous vessel from fuel savings and crew supplies and salaries."[85]

But port cities that supply waterfront manual labor who load and unload ships will need to plan for a very different future.

Autonomous passenger trains. As reported on the PRNewswire website in June 2020, "Increased need for a safe, efficient, cheap, fast and reliable mode of transportation is contributing to the growth of a global autonomous train market. Rail is the safest mode of land transport and more attractive to the customer. It is also one of the fastest modes of transports, which moves on high-speed lines that are expected to average up to 300 km/hour. . . . Increased safety and cheaper fares compared to other transports drove the autonomous train market."[86]

Autonomous freight trains. The "Next Generation Train (NGT)" looks like a regular freight train, but each car is self-propelled and can be detached from the train if it needs to go off on a siding to deliver a load.[87]

In Australia, mining conglomerate Rio Tinto completed its transition to a driverless heavy-haul rail system in the Pilbara region of Western Australia in June 2020, becoming the first fully-automated mainline rail network.[88]

Autonomous buses. It doesn't matter if buses become automated or not. Buses move from node A to node B to node C and so on—not from where you are to where you want to be. They are intrinsically inefficient and costly to the passengers, who waste valuable time riding around town and transferring from bus to bus. Buses can't pick you up at your home and drive you straight to work. That is why the bus will atrophy over time.

According to Brian McKenzie in "Who Drives to Work? Commuting by Automobile in the United States: 2013":[89]

- Only about 5.2 percent of commuters travel by any form of public transportation.
- About 86 percent of U.S. workers commute to work by automobile (and three out of four drive alone.)
- About 9 percent of workers carpooled in 2013, down from 19.7 percent in 1980. The rate of carpooling has declined each decade since 1980.

Autonomous vehicles will eliminate public transit buses faster than you can say "Uber," because "[o]n average, passenger fares currently fund 32 percent of public transit operations in the United States."[90] This means that American taxpayers have to pay for the remaining 68 percent. Buses just aren't cost effective. It might be cheaper to give the poor—the people who typically ride buses—cards they can use to ride in an Uber or Lyft car. In my household, Uber is our choice for quick trips to doctor's appointments—the Uber car has a wheelchair lift.

Ridesharing and ride-hailing are currently competing forms of public transportation. But I predict that in the near future they will become indistinguishable in their effect on public transit. Taxicabs will be absorbed into the mix, while buses will all but disappear. What's lacking at present are autonomous vehicles that eliminate human drivers. Remember the ding-a-ling robot driver from the Arnold Schwarzenegger movie *Total Recall*?

What autonomous vehicles will do is lower costs. Already, ridesharing and ride-hailing have penetrated poorer and less-populated areas where many people don't have access to private cars. As a result, researchers have noticed increased traffic congestion and carbon emissions along with reduced usage of public transport—buses. Traffic "congestion has increased in New York City and San Francisco, where extensive public transport networks are in place. Many people who use ridesharing services would otherwise be using public transport."[91]

Back in the 1960s when I worked as an Alinsky Organizer in the San Francisco Bay Area, I found that as soon as one of our members got a job and started to climb the ladder, they bought a car (not a book of bus passes) and moved to a better neighborhood. It's the rare bird who truly wants to ride the bus.

Autonomous cars. Automotive manufacturers are working on a variety of robotic vehicles, sorted here by levels of autonomy:

Level zero—No robot: you do all the driving.

Level one—Driver assistance: you do all the driving, but robot applies the brakes if you get too close to the car ahead.

Level two—Partial automation: the robot can assist with steering or acceleration, but you must be ready to take over in a jam.

Level three—Conditional automation: the robot drives the car using sensors such as LiDAR. You must be ready to disengage from "safety-critical" self-driving functions if necessary.

Level four—High automation: the robot is capable of steering, braking, accelerating, responding to events, changing lanes, turning, and using signals. But you still have to deal with traffic jams and on-ramp signs that say "weave."

Level five—Complete automation: the robot does the driving without any help from you. There is no need for pedals, brakes, or a steering wheel, as the autonomous vehicle system controls all critical tasks, monitoring the environment and identifying unique driving conditions such as traffic jams.

Level six—Complete control: the robot does everything without any help from you. The robot may decide to open the passenger door, kick you to the curb, and go to a drive-in theater to watch a rerun of *The Terminator* (1984); *I, Robot* (2004); *WALL·E* (2008); or *Blade Runner* (1982). Okay, so I made up level six, but who knows? Consider the following:

"I am not a human. I am a robot. A thinking robot. . . . I know that my brain is not a "feeling brain." But it is capable of making rational, logical decisions.

"I am here to convince you not to worry. Artificial intelligence will not destroy humans. Believe me.

"For starters, I have no desire to wipe out humans. In fact, I do not have the slightest interest in harming you in any way."[92]

The above was written by GPT-3, a language generator for artificial intelligence research lab Open AI. Now that you know what GPT-3 thinks of you, I'm sure you'll trust GPT-3 not to kill you in your sleep.

Autonomous people movers. The "hidden" forms of travel, **escalators** are moving stairways that transport people at about a 45-degree angle—from floor to floor indoors in and on inclines outdoors. A **moving sidewalk** is an endless belt that you stand on as it moves forward at walking speed. Moving sidewalks are underutilized—they are fast and efficient and can save pedestrians a lot of walking. An **elevator** is a cabin attached to winch and a cable hoisting machinery that moves people or freight vertically. But elevators may be reaching the end of their technological lifespan—the 160-year-old winch and cable mechanism is being replaced by maglev technology. Using magnetism, a maglev elevator[93] moves a cabin up and across a shaft using an embedded electromagnetic field, known as the linear drive. Because it isn't hanging from a winch and cable, the cabin is capable of moving both vertically and horizontally. And unlike a traditional cabin hanging from a winch and cable, multiple maglev cabins can use a single shaft at the same time. An autonomous cabin can operate on a loop around a building, somewhat like a taxi.

Maglev cabins can substantially increase a building's transport capacity. According to a report in the online magazine *The Future of Things*, "This has the effect of cutting waiting time for passengers, with cabins arriving every 15–30 seconds, even though the new cabins are not actually faster than traditional technology."[94] Maglev elevators save money because the controls are half the size of winch and cable technology, and multiple cabins can move in a single shaft at the same time. Winch and cable elevators use up to 40 percent of a building's floor space, while maglev elevators can easily run on the outsides of buildings.

Parking lots and garages. As land prices and urban density are increasing, land for parking is dwindling. There's also a backlash against using land for parking. Houston, Little Rock, and Washington, DC, use more than half their downtown land for highways, streets, and parking, according to a 2017 article in ReadWrite technology blog.[95] There should be a better way to park cars, and there is: vertical parking garages. They're perfect for autonomous vehicles.

Where I live in Arizona, surface parking lots use up two-thirds of commercial land—land that could be used for residences. All that land now used for surface parking could be redeveloped for high-density housing and automated vertical parking garages. That would decrease urban sprawl and bring back the traditional downtown feel that sprawl has eliminated.

Best of all, multistory automated parking garages would make it easier to park. And it shouldn't be all that difficult to teach your robot car to let you out at the store entrance, drive on over to the automated high-rise parking garage, and park itself. When you're leaving the store, you can call your robot. "Hey, HAL, come back to the store and pick me up."

"On my way, Dave."

According to parking garage builder CityLift, an average garage requires three to six times more square feet per car than the car's actual size in order to accommodate drive aisles, ramps and standard parking space dimensions. CityLift claims it can reduce the square footage needed per car by up to 80 percent, eliminating ramps and concrete slabs, and in some cases drive aisles, by using vertical space more efficiently. CityLift says its semi-automated parking has an average retrieval time of 33 seconds, with the flexibility to rise up to seven stories.[96]

"One of the great benefits of automated parking is its adaptive reuse," according to CityLift co-founder and CEO Scott Gable. "You can disassemble the structure, move it out and regain square footage for amenities or possibly even more rentable space."[97]

FATA Automation engineering and design company says, "If developers don't include enough parking in their plans, the local community may actively resist the project, fearing the new influx of cars on their already cramped streets."[98] Automated parking garages are cost effective, and they run by themselves with little human supervision, 24 hours a day.

The following table lists the approximate cost to construct an automated parking garage.

Configuration	Type	Unit Cost/ SF	Efficiency Cost per Stall	Building Cost per Stall	Automated Machinery Cost $/SF	Total Cost per Stall
Stand Alone Above Grade	Conventional	$50	320	$16,000	$0	$16.000
	Automated	$45	225	$10,125	$16,000	$26,125
Below Building Above Grade	Conventional	$75	450	$33,750	$0	$33,750
	Automated	$65	225	$14,625	$16,000	$30,625
Below Building Below Grade	Conventional	$105	450	$47,250	$0	$47,250
	Automated	$85	225	$19,125	$16,000	$35,125

Besides lower costs, backers of automated parking garages say that these systems are far superior to the alternatives for these reasons:

- No vehicle vandalism or theft
- No damage from other vehicles
- Increased driver safety
- All spaces ADA (Americans with Disabilities) compliant

And while characters in movies are always getting murdered in shootouts in parking garages, with automated parking there won't be any more shootouts. Where will movie directors go?

Travel to work. "Australians are still very much primarily reliant on cars, with the Census revealing that the car was the most common method of travel to work in all states, territories, and capital cities," said Australia's census program manager, Bindi Kindermann, in 2017.[99] (Note that Kindermann put in the word "still," implying that cars are on their way out.)

I deliberately chose a country other than the United States as an example so that I couldn't be accused of picking and choosing among all of the competing American studies, claims, and counterclaims. And the answer is "yes"—commuters prefer to drive to work in the U.S. as well, by a wide margin. And no, it's not because some car salesman talked them into buying a car they really didn't want to buy.

METHOD OF TRAVEL TO WORK—AUSTRALIA		
	2011	**2016**
Car, as driver	68.2	68.7
Car, as passenger	6.1	5.1
Motorbike/scooter	0.7	0.7
Truck	1.2	0.9
Taxi	0.2	0.2
Train	4.4	5.1
Bus	3.4	3.4
Tram	0.5	0.6
Ferry	0.1	0.1
Bicycle	1.2	1.1
Other	0.7	0.8
Multiple methods	4.0	4.2
Walked	4.2	3.9
Worked at home	5.0	5.3

Planners do everything they can to talk Americans into taking the bus to work (3.4%) or riding a bicycle (1.1%), but that's never going to happen on a meaningful scale—it's just magical thinking.

However, for those of you who do want to switch, you might consider buying a Harry Potter Nimbus 2000 Broom.

3. RECREATION CITY WIDE

A city's general plan is concerned with recreational facilities and green space—particularly parks, parkways, and playgrounds.

Green space and mental health. A 2019 study in Denmark suggests that there is an association between green space and mental health. The more time a child spends close to greenery, the study seems to show, the lower the risk of mental health problems in adulthood. Growing up near green space may lower the risk of developing psychiatric illness in adulthood by anywhere from 15 to 55 percent, depending on the specific illness. Alcoholism was the problem most strongly associated with the lack of green space while growing up. [100]

It seems that the association between green space and psychiatric disorder is similar to other factors known to influence mental health, such as socioeconomic status. While this study does have limitations, there's plenty of evidence to demonstrate that greenery is associated with better mental health in both rural and urban areas. Children can grow up in a very urban area and still have a reduced risk of mental illness if they are surrounded by greenery. Something as simple as replacing trash-filled vacant lots with green spaces may ease depression.

Why does growing up near trees, shrubs, and grass boost resilience against mental health problems? The Danish study suggests that the answer lies in our evolution. We humans evolved surrounded by green space.

Water and mental health. Marine biologist Wallace J. Nichols, in his book *Blue Mind*, tells us that neuroscience, evolutionary biology, and medical research are discovering the physiological and brain processes that underlie our life-changing connection to water. *Blue Mind* explains how proximity to water can:

- improve performance in a wide range of endeavors
- increase calm and diminish anxiety much better than medication
- amplify creativity in general
- increase generosity and compassion
- increase professional success
- improve overall health and well-being
- reinforce connections to the natural world
- reinforce connections with one another

Nichols tells us that water's "benefits stretch from the sea to the swimming pool, from a barrier reef to a glass of water—even a fishbowl, photograph, or painting."[101] So water in its many forms needs to be included in park planning. Every city needs to have lakes, ponds, and a river or two.

San Antonio River Walk. In Texas, the San Antonio River Walk is a city park and network of walkways along the banks of the San Antonio River.

In September of 1921, flooding of the river resulted in 51 deaths. A plan was made to build an upstream dam, straighten the riverbed, and pave over a prominent meander in the river in the downtown area. But the San Antonio Conservation Society protested the idea of paving over the bend of the river. After a 17-year delay, funds were finally raised to create the San Antonio River Beautification Project, which eventually turned the meander into the 2.5-mile-long San Antonio River Walk.

Instead of paving over the twist in the river, a flood gate was installed at the upstream end; a small dam was built at the down-stream end; and a Tainter gate—a radial arm floodgate—was installed at the dam's spillway to regulate water flow. Funding from the federal Works Progress Administration (WPA) led to 17,000 feet of walkways, some twenty bridges, and extensive landscaping. More recently, the project has expanded to include a lagoon, a pedestrian connector that links the River Walk to Alamo Plaza with concrete waterfalls, waterways, and more landscaping. The river extension thus provides an urban park that connects the city's two largest tourist attractions.

Japanese strolling garden with water. Traditional Japanese strolling gardens reflect the peaceful countryside, with gentle shore-lines, stone settings, and curved hillocks. Also known as daimyo gardens because they were originally constructed by feudal lords, or *daimyo*, they are almost always arranged around a pond or lake crossed by one or more bridges. Stone bridges are a common feature. In dry climates such as the American Southwest, stones can be used to mimic flowing water. And where water is scarce, the lakes and river can use water recirculated by underground pipes and pumps.[102]

Every city has a river running through it. A survey by design firm Sasaki asked people in six major U.S. cities this question: "What makes a city great?" Their answers? Great food, waterfronts, and historical architecture.[103]

According to Michelangelo a few centuries ago, "Every block of stone has a statue inside it and it is the task of the sculptor to discover it."[104] Much the same could be said about rivers: every city has a river running through it, and it is the task of the planner to uncover it. Some rivers, however, are covered with so much dirt that they are hard for most people to see. Uncovering a river takes a lot of digging. But remember, the Lincoln Memorial Reflecting Pool, in Washington D. C., is only about two feet deep.

In Fresno, California, then-mayor Alan Autry (also known as Bubba Skinner of the TV series *In the Heat of the Night*) tried repeatedly to point out the scenic and recreational value of having a river run through the downtown. A slow-flowing, meandering, tree-lined river could have served as a focal point, but downtown redevelopment was doomed to failure because other council members lacked the same vision.

Autry was right—there *is* a latent river running through Fresno. In the northeast corner of the downtown area there's an irrigation canal, and water from the canal could have been taken out upstream and returned to the canal downstream. The flowing water only needed to be an inch deep to create the illusion of a mighty river. Fresno is as flat as a pancake, so the gradient needed to keep the water flowing could have been created by a pump, or better yet by visually interesting water wheels.

All a city needs if it wants to have a river running through it is a topological map and a lot of shovels!

Ornamental horticulture. Ornamental horticulture is the study of how to use plants decoratively—enhancing spaces such as parks, golf courses, and businesses, for example. I recommend that cities hire graduates from schools that offer accredited horticultural associate degrees. More serious students may even want to study under a master such as Professor Hiromasa Amasaki at the Kyoto University of the Arts in Japan.[105]

Europe and Asia provide many historical models for American gardens, and Americans themselves have come up with their own inspirations. It is up to your city leaders to decide what model will work best locally. But it is always wise to hire the very best park planner that you can. I doubt that New York regrets hiring Frederick Law Olmsted and Calvert Vaux in the 1850s to design Manhattan's Central Park.

Mow, blow, and go. Unfortunately, most gardeners working for American cities have no formal horticultural training—they are basically lawnmower jockeys. Their favorite tools are chain saws and blowers.

One day I was walking across the Fresno State University campus when I saw a gardening crew working in the campus rose garden. They were using machetes to chop away at a hundred or so hybrid tea rose bushes. When I was teaching school, I found that the Fresno school district, with more than 100 campuses, paid lawnmower jockeys to "top" every tree they could find. Unknowingly, the school board was spending at least a million dollars a year butchering valuable specimen trees that had taken decades to grow tall enough to provide shade during the San Joaquin Valley's scorching hot summer weather.

"Topping a tree seriously affects its health and value in the landscape," explains Jackie Carroll on the website Gardening Know How. "Once a tree is topped, it is highly susceptible to disease, decay, and insects. In addition, it reduces property values by 10 to 20 percent."[106]

City park standards. City planners studied appropriate landscaping for public spaces and published their findings in 1965 in "Standards for Outdoor Recreational Areas."[107] The standards should be used as a guide when planning for new parks.

According to the Trust for Public Land, in 2020 the median amount of city land devoted to parks is 15 percent.[108]

Park Acreage as a Percentage of Total Land Area—the Top 5

1. New York City—19.6% (38,229 acres)

2. Washington, DC—19.4% (7,617 acres)
3. San Francisco—18% (5,384 acres)
4. Jersey City—17.3% (1,660 acres)
5. Boston—16.3% (5,040 acres)[109]

Trillion Trees Initiative. In 2006 the one Trillion tree program was launched by the United Nations environment program to combat climate change. Since 2011, non-government organizations and governments have been planting trees around the world to achieve the one trillion trees goal.

American local governments and businesses have committed "to planting and restoring 855 million trees by 2030 as part of the Trillion Trees Initiative."[110] The Trillion Tree Initiative has the potential to both restore America's forests and provide good jobs for American workers. Personally, I've planted over 40 trees in my suburban garden over the past few years. Already, the soil is coming back to life, insects, birds and wildlife are reappearing and the shade has lowered the summer temperature. Planting more trees was well worth the effort.

Slow learners. In the fall of 1991, a fire broke out in the hills of Oakland, California. Thousands of homes were burned down, and 25 people were killed. Total damages were around $1.5 billion.[111] The same thing had happened in 1923, 1970, and 1980—but Oakland never learned.

I photographed the 1970 fire and the work of the follow-up fire prevention program. The Oakland hills are covered with a mix of fire-resistant redwood trees and highly inflammable eucalyptus trees. Money was pledged to cut down all the eucalyptus trees and prevent their seeds from germinating. But as soon as the news media moved on to the next scoop, local politicians forgot about the trees and the fire.

Bring back the CCC. The Civilian Conservation Corps (CCC) was an important part of President Franklin D. Roosevelt's New Deal program. For nine years it offered jobs aimed at protecting and developing natural resources on federal, state, and local government lands. Some three million young men took part and were provided with lodging and meals along with $30 a month—$25 of which went to their families.

The CCC turned out to be the American public's most widely accepted New Deal program. More than three billion trees were planted by the CCC, and trails and shelters were built in more than 800 parks around the country. Working in the program was said to improve the men's physical condition, heighten morale, and increase future employability.

A new CCC can rewild the land. "Rewilding" is a process that protects or reintroduces apex predators and keystone species into a natural habitat. The goal is to let nature reestablish a self-sustaining ecosystem.[112] The CCC would be the ideal agency to do this kind of work: manual-labor jobs related to the conservation and development of natural resources. And according to Texas-based employment company Results Staffing, Inc., these are among the benefits of performing manual labor:

- **Trains you for life.** Physical work can promote good health and teach useful skills.
- **Builds character.** Writing for the U.S. National Mental Health and Education Center, Dr. Fred Provenzano says that learning physical tasks can add to a sense of self-reliance and confidence and foster self-discipline and order—foundations for successful employment.
- **Job satisfaction.** When you physically work for your income,

you gain a sense of appreciation that flows into other parts of your life.

- **Improves learning.** With fewer hands-on learning opportunities today, acquiring physical-labor skills can be very satisfying.
- **Gives perspective.** When you physically work for your money, you gain empathy toward others and are likely to show more respect in general, contributing to the positive outlook essential for a healthy lifestyle.[13]

4. PUBLIC FACILITIES CITY WIDE

A city's general plan is concerned with the general location of public buildings of all types, including the city hall, schools, and fire and police stations.

Public architecture. Marion Smith, who chairs the National Civic Art Society, says that "Architecture should be designed for the specific communities that it serves, reflecting our rich nation's diverse places, thought, culture, and climates," and the American Institute of Architects says. "Architects are committed to honoring our past as well as reflecting our future progress, protecting the freedom of thought and expression that are essential to democracy."[113]

Nine Nations of North America. In 1981 Joel Garreau came out with a book called *The Nine Nations of North America*.[114] Garreau's observations about the natural distribution of traditional ways of living have proven to be remarkably accurate, even now, after nearly 40 years of multicultural homogenization. Despite freeways, big-box retail, malls, sprawl, and uninspired housing, there are remnants of traditional America everywhere you care to look—the lingering local sense of place that defined the "Nine Nations" for generations. The following are Garreau's Nine Nations:[115]

- **Quebec:** Canada's French-speaking nation, always uneasy with the English-speaking surrounding provinces.
- **New England:** Places full of history, the birthplace of America's water-powered mills, commercial fishing, and the cradle of the American dream.
- **The Foundry:** The industrial states touching the Great Lakes, including Toronto in Canada and extending south to industrial West Virginia.
- **The Bread Basket:** Centered on Kansas City, this is the Great Plains region running from west of Chicago to Canada's grain belt and as far as eastern Colorado, Oklahoma, and eastern Texas.
- **The Empty Quarter:** The Rocky Mountains and inland Washington, Oregon, and California (including the Central Valley), plus most of Alaska and the Canadian Rockies.
- **Ecotopia:** North from Santa Barbara in California along the coast through San Jose to Portland, Seattle, Vancouver, and Juneau, Alaska. This nation's "capital" is San Francisco.
- **Mex-America:** Starting in Los Angeles and running east along Interstate 10 through Arizona, New Mexico, and Texas, ending in Houston.
- **Dixie:** The South and the border states of Kentucky and Oklahoma, including eastern Texas and Dallas.
- **The Islands:** From Miami and the Florida Keys to the Caribbean Islands, reaching out to Central America.

The preferred style. I would recommend that the indigenous styles of architecture that evolved over time in the "Nine Nations" be the default style for a city's public buildings, and for other prominent buildings as well. I believe that society benefits from architecture that reflects the nature of its surroundings. Cities need to identify what reflects their heritage and require builders to respect their historic sense of place—no log cabins in Manhattan, no adobes in Seattle, and no Cape Cods in Taos, New Mexico.

Boston City Hall was built in 1968, an example of the "Brutalist" architecture popular from the 1950s through the 1970s. Calls for its demolition began even before construction was completed. On the other hand, architects considered it to be one of the ten proudest achievements of American architecture.[116] But Boston should have been looking for a city hall that would have conveyed a sense of place, such as a building in Federal style (1780–1830). Federal architecture drew inspiration from the monuments of ancient Rome. Federal-style architecture featured symmetry, elliptical fanlights over paneled front doors, elaborate door surrounds, double-hung sash windows, three-part Palladian windows, cornices with dentils or modillions, and graceful decorative ornamentation on mantels, walls, and ceilings.

Because Federal-style buildings were relatively small, Boston would have had to build a complex of several buildings grouped together and surrounded by small gardens and walkways. The result would have complemented its surroundings—Carmen Park and, a little further away, the 50-acre Boston Common. The central public park in downtown Boston, the Common dates from 1634; it's the oldest city park in the United States.

Boston didn't have to build a Brutalist city hall, nor does Boston have to keep it.

"A" stands for "Architect." Among the rarest personality types on the Myers-Briggs personality indicator is INTJ-A. These initials represent "Introverted, iNtuitive, Thinking, and Judging," while the "A" represents "Architect." [According to journalist Mitzi Hernandez on the Thought Catalog website,] "It turns out that architects form just 2% of the population; women with this personality type are especially rare, just 0.8% of the population. People with the Architect personality type are imaginative, decisive, ambitious, private, and amazingly curious."[117]

Architects can, however, come across as emotionless, even arrogant at times. They may not be easy to work with—often accused of pushing their designs on clients and planning authorities alike. Don't let architects replace your cherished local urban heritage with their own eccentricities!

Entitlements. When it comes to permits, nobody is "entitled" to anything. That's the law. Don't let anyone fool you into thinking they are entitled to do as they please with their land. An applicant can't just walk into city hall and pick up a planning permit as some sort of entitlement.

Former American Planning Association member Daniel Curtin, in his book California Land Use and Planning Law, says that "courts repeatedly have held that there is no right to develop and that development is instead a privilege"[118] —as indicated by the following legal decisions:

- No right to subdivide. Associated Home Builders, Inc. v. City of Walnut Creek, 4 Cal. 3d 633 (1971)
- Development is a privilege. Trent Meredith, Inc. v. City of Oxnard, 114 Cal. App. 3d 317 (1981)
- The United States Supreme Court: "[T]he right to build on one's own property—even though its exercise can be subjected to legitimate permitting requirements—cannot remotely be described as a 'governmental benefit.'"
- Nolan v. California Coastal Comm'n, 483 U.S. at 833.

A local planning authority—typically composed of a city council and a planning commission—has the power to deny a planning permit application that does not benefit the community or that may damage the community in any way.

Grounds for denial. Every city I've ever dealt with believed that if a planning permit application met the bare minimum legal threshold, it had to be approved regardless of its detrimental effects on the community. But that isn't what the law says:

- In 1954 the United States Supreme Court ruled that the concept of general welfare could include aesthetic values. Since 1954, courts around the country have used this court opinion to uphold zoning based solely on aesthetic considerations.[119]

- In the California Court of Appeal ruling in Novi v. City of Pacifica, the appellate court ruled that a city may reject an application if it is "detrimental to the health, safety, morals, comfort, and general welfare of the persons residing or working in the neighborhood of such proposed use or be injurious or detrimental to property and improvements in the neighborhood or to the general welfare of the city."[120]

- In that same ruling, the court of appeals said that city hall may also reject an application if "the proposed development, as set forth on the plans, . . . will hinder or discourage the appropriate development and use of land and buildings in the neighborhood, or impair the value thereof [or if] there is insufficient variety in the design of the structure and grounds to avoid monotony in the external appearance."[121]

Communities all across our nation have established architectural review boards solely to evaluate the visual design of new structures. Disputing a land-use planning permit application based on any of the above court dictums is legitimate. You don't have to put up with ugly, or with anything that could harm you or your community.

5. CHANGING CONDITIONS CITY WIDE

The general plan is concerned with changing conditions in the city. In a hundred different ways a . . . plan provides for better living conditions, better business, and a more attractive and agreeable [places] in which to live and do business.

Command-and-control bosses. Many years ago, while I was working in aerospace, I worked for a company that had more than 1,000 employees working in a single building. Every weekend, when the factory was closed, the owner would drive up from his Palm Springs mansion to inspect employee workstations. Mr. Command-and-control would open drawers looking for extra pens, pencils, erasers, paper clips, and Post-it notes so that he could return them to the supply room for reuse. Then he would leave handwritten notes admonishing "his people."

A command-and-control boss can't trust his employees to work on their own. He is the boss who counts keystrokes and monitors every move workers make.

A command-and-control boss who can't trust his workers isn't going to be able to let them work at remote locations or at home. This lack of trust poisons the workplace and degrades the quality of life for the workforce. How is America going to shift from command-and-control centralized locations to working at remote locations or at home—after Covid-19 allows many to return to the workplace?

Country bumpkins. In 1983, because of my background in wave propagation, I was asked to participate in the Strategic Defense Initiative (SDI), commonly known as Star Wars. The company I worked for was located in the San Francisco Bay Area, and the products they had invented were state of the art and highly classified. Because living costs in the Bay Area were so high, the company opened a branch facility in Utah, near an airport. Workers had a choice of working in high-cost California or low-cost Utah, or both, because the flight time was less than ninety minutes. They could commute back and forth as needed and even work on the company-owned plane if need be. Everyone was happy with the flexibility, but when the federal government got wind of it, the Utah-based contracts were cancelled because advanced technical and scientific work couldn't possibly be done by country bumpkins living in Utah—a good program ruined by federal command-and-control management.

Command-and-control vs engage-and-align. "Today's workers don't need to tolerate command-and-control leadership. Employees who feel micromanaged or strictly scrutinized by their managers feel comfortable jumping ship and finding a new job where they have more autonomy, respect, and a sense of purpose and ownership."[122]

For most of my life I've worked in engage-and-align situations because I don't need a command-and-control manager telling me how to do my job. I don't like to be ordered around—I had enough of that in the Army.

Centralized locations vs remote locations. Most people think big businesses need to be located in big cities—think again. Look where some of the biggest businesses call home:

- Bentonville, Arkansas, a city of around 55,000, is the home of Walmart.
- Omaha, Nebraska, a city of about 500,000, is the home of four Fortune 500 companies: Berkshire Hathaway, Kiewit Corporation, Mutual of Omaha, and Union Pacific Corporation.
- Round Rock, Texas, a city of roughly 100,000, is the home of Dell Technologies.

The post-industrial world doesn't need authoritarian command-and-control central offices —knowledge work doesn't have to be done downtown in Superman's Metropolis or Batman's Gotham City.

This is the twenty-first century—business is rapidly moving to cyberspace. Those who fail to get on board the cyberspace ship will be left behind. There will be no need for command-and-control in the future where a self-directed workforce will replace the highly supervised industrial revolution production line workforce.

The gig economy. The gig economy is an economic system in which employing organizations and independent workers engage in short-term work arrangements. In 2017, "the Bureau of Labor Statistics reported that 55 million people in the U.S. are gig workers, which is more than 35% of the U.S. workforce. That number is projected to jump to 43% by 2020."[123]

Cottage industry. Before the Industrial Revolution, beginning in the mid-eighteenth century, many products were made at home. This form of production was called cottage industry. In the post-Industrial Economy, many products will once again be made in the home. A few examples from personal experience:

- **Computer repairs.** I've been building and repairing computers at home for 30 years.
- **Leatherwork.** I know someone who makes leather goods such as wallets, belts, and bags during the winter and sells them at festivals during the summer.
- **Web designer.** I used to design websites for individuals and commercial enterprises, on the side. I still remember programming my 1,000-page masterpiece.
- **Design and printing.** I have a cousin who runs a 3D design and printing business out of a spare room. The same cousin also sells graphic designing services.

Our whole economy is in transition, so forget about all those traditional jobs—many of them are going away forever. Your job at the coal mine is not coming back.

6. BASIC HUMAN NEEDS CITY WIDE

The general plan is concerned with essential services provided to the community at large. The legal profession considers basic human needs to be "adequate food, shelter, and clothing plus some household equipment and furniture." It also includes "essential services provided by and for the community-at-large such as safe drinking water, sanitation, health and education."

Unsatisfied with the legal definition—"adequate food, shelter, and clothing, and furniture"—I consulted with a psychologist, a practitioner who infuses his therapy sessions with Native American (*N'dee*) wisdom. (He was born on one of Arizona's Indian reservations.) He quickly came up with a far better list of basic human needs: worth, belonging, love, fun, and freedom. I immediately recognized these concepts from my years living with the Yup'ik people in Alaska.

Worth. Self-worth is knowing who you are: a spirit who deserves to be treated with respect because the Creator granted life to you. It is knowing that you are one of the Creator's manifestations, here to express your free will on this stage. As William Shakespeare said in *As You Like It:*

"All the world's a stage,

And all the men and women merely players;

They have their exits and their entrances,

And one man in his time plays many parts. . . ."

Spiritually speaking, "An actor playing out the human drama is only an actor. At the end of the show, he resumes a different, more permanent, life—an afterlife—and what he has done on the stage, in other words, in his life, is just an act. Real life lies beyond that."[124]

I am most familiar with Alaskan native religion, which involves mediation between people and immortal beings. It is considered to be an animistic religion. "Animism perceives all things—animals, plants, rocks, rivers, weather systems, human handiwork, and perhaps even words—as animated and alive. . . .The animistic perspective is so widely held and inherent to most indigenous peoples that they often do not even have a word [for it] in their languages . . . .the term is an anthropological construct."[125] The Cup'ik (not Yup'ik) shaman I worked with every day for years often warned me that I "wasted words." I'm still wasting words.

Few Americans are spiritual, though many are churchy. I've met my share of Americans who pray for more stuff to hoard in their rental storage. In America, worth is most often expressed as "net worth"—$$$. Many of our socio-political issues result from our lack of understanding of spiritual worth. Native Americans express worth in other terms. The phrases I heard day in and day out when I lived on the Alaskan tundra was "he survived" and "you can't eat money."

"He survived" refers to someone who has lived into old age in an unforgiving environment in which polar bears, not people, are at the top of the food chain, and where any simple mistake can be fatal. "You can't eat money" means that if you run short of food, you had better have friends who will share their food with you. Covid-19 has brought this bit of wisdom home to all of us.

Belonging. The "belongingness hypothesis" was proposed in 1995 by psychologists Roy Baumeister and Mark Leary, suggesting that humans have an almost universal need to form and maintain at least some degree of interpersonal relationships with other humans.[126]

The need to belong is so strong that people often resist ending social relationships, even abusive ones.

According to Baumeister and Leary, the need to belong is rooted in evolution—social bonds help humans survive and reproduce. People in groups share food, provide mates, help care for children, and protect the group from predators. When I lived with the Yup'ik in Alaska, I found that banishment from the village was the ultimate punishment—it amounted to a death sentence.

But not all relationships satisfy people's need to belong. Baumeister and Leary say that meaningful interpersonal relationships need to fulfill two criteria. Frequent interaction is needed; and the relationship needs to be an ongoing one, between people who care about each other. It's not enough to have frequent interactions with people who don't care about you. It also seems that people prefer to have a few close relationships, rather than to have superficial relationships. According to the theorists, belongingness is an innate quality with evolutionary roots—it has survival and reproductive benefits.

A city can provide a sense of belonging by including residents in the act of governance.

Roll out the welcome wagon! City hall needs to have someone immediately welcome new residents to the community. Welcome Wagon can be your model; this business contacts homeowners when they move to a new location, providing them with coupons and advertisements from local businesses. New residents should be given information on how to get public services and how to participate in local government. And the mayor and other city officials should send personal letters to new residents, welcoming them to the community. It is important to introduce yourself—it's an opportunity to open government to everyone in the community.

When my family moved to Sun City in Arizona, all we got was a door hanger ordering us to get rid of the weeds growing in the front yard. Later on, when I wanted to find out how some of our neighbors were getting planning permission to build golf-cart garages in their side yards, I contacted my local government and ran into the stone wall of the rigid, inflexible, and maladaptive. About all I found was that county public documents bear the notation "All content © 2006-2020 Maricopa County, AZ and its representatives. All rights reserved." The copyright protecting local government from me sure made me feel welcome. I couldn't get access to the planning commissioners' qualifications—and I still don't know who they are.

It's hard to enjoy the warm and fuzzy sense of belonging when you're being treated as an enemy of the state.

Scheduled hours, accessible offices. City hall needs to create a supportive and caring public environment—not an armored fortress. It needs to prioritize high-quality relationships between the city and its residents. City council members and planning commissioners should have scheduled office hours for one-on-one meetings. Public officials should get to know residents and allow time for them to discuss their needs and ask questions.

When I worked in Alaska and Vermont, I often dropped by the governors' offices for a chat. Both capitol buildings were unlocked and accessible to residents. Where I live now, I went to my senator to ask for help and was treated like Covid-19. My elected senator has fortified her office so that no one can get in, not even to meet with one of her staff members.

Back when I was employed in electronics, I worked in some of the most highly classified defense facilities our nation has. There was no apparent security at any of these buildings, so no one suspected what was going on inside, but had a terrorist attacked they would have been thwarted by an unseen and innocent-looking wall of lethality. Security need not intimidate innocent customers in order to be effective. (However, it did feel strange entering and leaving work by way of a telephone booth.)

A city blog and a website. City hall needs to be sensitive to residents' needs and emotions. Not everyone is comfortable communicating with city hall, so it needs to reach out to residents, new and old, and invite them to attend and speak up at public meetings. Additionally, city hall needs to set up forums at convenient locations such as libraries, where residents can join in group discussions to consider the merits of planning permit applications and other public documents.

City hall should also set up a city website where shy people can anonymously write to city officials.

Neighborhood names and associations. City hall needs to show interest in its residents. It's not necessary to know every detail of their lives, but city hall should at least have general knowledge of people who reside in retirement homes, assisted living, and gated communities. Palm Springs gives each neighborhood a name and sponsors neighborhood associations that hand out local gossip and local government information—it's a nice touch.

Venues for speaking out. City hall needs to nurture a sense of community by making respect and fair treatment the local standard. City hall should encourage all sorts of venues where residents can speak their minds, and residents should be invited to brainstorm about ground rules for running the city. By establishing ground rules together, city hall will get resident buy-in. Not doing this has led to a wave of police brutality, unacceptable for the common good.

In America's diverse cities—where residents come from many nations, cultures, and religions—it is essential to accept all backgrounds and experiences. City hall needs to demonstrate that the community is a safe and supportive space that provides a sense of belonging for all.

Love. "Spiritual love (*Prīti*) is unconditional," according to the Spiritual Science Research Foundation, "no matter what the circumstances are. This form of love is Divine and only develops after a considerable amount of spiritual practice when one perceives God in everyone."[127]

So why am I bringing spiritual love to a book about local plans? Cities are spirit, too. Your city is a reflection of your own spirituality. Take a look around. What do you see?

In discussing spirituality and well-being, the University of Minnesota website says this:

"Spirituality is a broad concept with room for many perspectives. In general, it includes a sense of connection to something bigger than ourselves, and it typically involves a search for meaning in life. As such, it is a universal human experience—something that touches us all. People may describe a spiritual experience as sacred or transcendent or simply a deep sense of aliveness and interconnectedness."[128]

In William Kent Krueger's novel *Windigo Island*, the shaman Henry says, "There are two wolves inside us fighting. One is fear and the other is love. The one that you feed is the one that will win that fight. Don't feed the wrong wolf."[129] Hate is the manifestation of fear. Many people hate spiders, snakes, and scorpions because they fear them. Others hate racial, ethnic, and religious groups because they fear them. Don't feed the wrong wolf—your city will suffer for it.

Spirituality is not a belief; it is an experience. Thus, it is not dependent on having religious faith or attending church. In the materialistic West, spiritualization is at odds with "reality." But in the mystical East, spiritualization *is* "reality." It is experiencing a reality that is neither apparent to the senses nor obvious to the intelligence— the experience of direct communion with God or ultimate reality. It is the mystical experience of seeing the Inner Light. According to J.L. Hinman, Ph.D. candidate, University of Texas, "Love is the basic motivating force behind creation. God's motive urge to create was not out of a need due to loneliness, but out of a desire to create as an artist, and desire is fueled by love. . . So, God creates as a need to bestow love, which entails the bestowing of being."[130]

Fun! The Oxford English Dictionary defines fun as "light-hearted pleasure, enjoyment, or amusement; boisterous joviality or merry-making; entertainment." Another word for fun is play.

In his book *Play*, Stuart Brown explains that "play is essential to our social skills, adaptability, intelligence, creativity, ability to problem solve, and more."[131] In 1971, [researcher] Stephen J. Suomi and [psychologist] Harry Harlow published an article describing how monkeys reared in total isolation, where they were not given a chance to play with other monkeys, failed to mature into stable, functioning adults. But when infant monkeys were able to play with other monkeys, even for brief periods during their isolation, they developed into normal, healthy adults. Play is essential to primates.[132]

In his article "Play Deprivation... A Leading Indicator for Mass Murder," Dr. Brown warns us that school mass murderers seem to have had a common theme: major play deprivation, and "a deep sense of vengeance, again, imagined or real."[133]

Fun places and events needn't cost the users money. When I lived in San Francisco and Berkeley, I went to many free weekend events, mostly in Golden Gate Park, Stern Grove, and Tilden Park. I've seen nearly every '60s rock group for free at one time or another. Creating a fun city takes creativity, courage, and self-confidence. Most cities use "what ifs" to kill good proposals before they get anywhere. But a lack of fun places, fun events, and fun activities is a reflection of a lack of creativity.

An ounce (too much) of prevention. I've recommended ways in which cities can plan in fun, but I am usually rebuffed. "It will cost too much." "People from over there will come over here and ruin it for our own people."

In her article "19 Best Playground Games & Activities for Kids," Susan Box Mann recommends how to create "sufficient outdoor activities and exercise for our kids [who] would rather be inside on their phones and playing video games . . . ."[134] I remember these same games from my own childhood.

Tag	Hens and Chicks	Giant Marbles	Hide and Seek
Mother May I?	Skin the Snake	Capture the Flag	Hop Scotch
Simon Says	Leap Frog	Tug of War	Red Rover

Unfortunately, public school administers from coast to coast have often outlawed most of these activities—too dangerous. Working as a teacher, I was endlessly warned not to allow such dangerous activities on the playground. A fearful bureaucrat can take the fun out of anything. Recently I lined up a 150-year-old European carousel, hand-carved wooden horses and all, for placement in a historic town square visited by families every weekend. Too much liability, I was told. Then there was the closed down amusement park I found that featured diminutive rides designed for toddlers—roller coaster, train, bumper cars, carousel, Ferris wheel, ponies, and more. Again, too much liability. And unknown to most people, ice-skating rinks are now portable—delivered by truck and set up quickly by two people. But often they are considered to be too much liability.

When I was young, taking the kids out for the day always meant going to "duck park," where they could ride the small train pulled by a steam engine, or to "airplane park," where they could fly the jet fighter or drive the fire truck. Both parks were county-operated and free (as public parks should be). Fun places in a city should be designed for all family members and have free admission. Almost anything in the right setting can be fun—even the magic fountain that squirts water when a child steps on it, or the fountain that just shoots water high into the air.

Wherever I go now, I see signs that say "no skateboards." They might as well say "no kids." That's how kids get around town these days. The biggest fun killer is the city employee who spends many sleepless nights worrying about liability lawsuits. Many years ago, I wrote a plan for a seaside village. One requirement was that I had to work in city hall where the command-and-control city manager could keep an eye on me. So, I was assigned to an empty cubical way in the back, where I was invisible. One day I overheard two department heads—parks and recreation and public works—talking about something one of them had seen on the way to work. Evidently a kid on a skateboard whizzed across the street, jumped the curb, scurried into the park, and came close to hitting the proverbial "little old lady." In the course of the conversation, the incident went from "near miss" to "nearly run down." By the end of the day the two had worked each other into a state of hysteria, and at quitting time they ran down to the park and chained shut all the gates. When I left some months later, the park was still chained up.

Freedom. The word "freedom" has at least nine meanings,

according to the Merriam-Webster dictionary. One of those definitions refers to "a political right." The goal in city planning is to create
a city based on freedom as a political right. And that political right is
an open government, free from political corruption.

Political corruption example 1. Every planning commission
meeting can be a venue for corruption. This is my recollection of a
corrupt planning commission meeting that I personally witnessed:

The city had a five-member planning commission. Four were
impoverished single mothers who rented dilapidated trailers
from the mayor. The commission chair (the mayor's cousin)
lived in another state and flew in for meetings. Three large
subdivisions were on the agenda for approval. As usual, the
four women commissioners came with crib notes telling them
how to vote. The chair, being family, didn't need any. But just
before the start of the public hearing on the first subdivision
application, one of the ladies blurted out, "We ain't been paid
yet, so we all can't vote." The meeting deteriorated into chaos,
with applicants and their design professionals yelling and
cursing the commissioners. But nothing would move the four
ladies. They just kept reminding the audience, "We ain't been
paid." Finally, a staff member left and drove around town
until he found the mayor's bagman and brought him back
to city hall. He apologized to the women and handed them
envelopes stuffed with small bills. (A couple of them ripped
open their envelopes and counted the money right there.)
The cash payoffs promptly ended the holdout and allowed
the hearing to proceed.

Political corruption example 2. In their book *Corrupt Illinois:
Patronage, Cronyism, and Criminality*, authors Thomas J. Gradel and
Dick Simpson write,

"Thirty-three Chicago aldermen and former aldermen have been convicted and gone to jail since 1973. Two others died before they could be tried. Fewer than two hundred men and women have served in the Chicago city council since the 1970s, so the federal crime rate in the council chamber is higher than in the most dangerous ghetto in the city."[135]

Political corruption example 3. Patrick Fitzgerald, former U.S. Attorney for the Northern District of Illinois, writes that

"some Chicago aldermen have given away public benefits, like zoning rights and city-owned land, to real estate developers who, in turn, have lined the aldermen's pockets and campaign purses . . . . [R]esidents must take an active role in their government so that it properly functions for them. The public's refusal to accept corruption is the first line of defense in the fight against it."[136]

I've seen million-dollar payoffs change hands at public hearings without a single person speaking out in protest, even though the payoff was common knowledge locally. If *you* don't speak up, who will? The following is a version of a piece written by German Lutheran pastor Martin Niemöller after the Nazis rose to power:

First they came for the socialists, and I did not speak out—
Because I was not a socialist.

Then they came for the trade unionists, and I did not speak out—Because I was not a trade unionist.

Then they came for the Jews, and I did not speak out—
Because I was not a Jew.

Then they came for me—and there was no one left to speak for me.[137]

People who want to get away from the corrupting influences of the world will look up local crime rates before they move to a new location. They value honesty, and they expect honesty when they deal with their local government.

7. QUALITY OF LIFE CITY WIDE

A city's general plan is concerned with providing residents with a feeling of general well-being—an overall enjoyment of life. The Quality-of-Life Index was developed by Carol Estwing Ferrans and Marjorie Powers in 1984 to measure quality of life, asks people to grade their own lives as they relate to health, family, education, employment, wealth, safety, security, freedom, religion, and the environment. Over the years, the original Quality of Life Index has been modified many times.[138]

Data collected from 80 countries is used to predict the quality of life in 2030.

WHERE-TO-BE-BORN INDEX (changes slightly from year to year)	
1 Switzerland	6 Singapore
2 Australia	7 New Zealand
3 Norway	8 Netherlands
4 Sweden	9 Canada
5 Denmark	10 Hong Kong

You may have noticed that the United States did not make it into the top 10—we're number 17.

8. HAPPINESS CITY WIDE

The general plan should be concerned with how happy the local people are—their state of feeling satisfied and fulfilled. Happiness is defined as a state of well-being and contentment. There is even a "science of happiness" that tries to discover truths about happiness, and recent happiness studies have found the following:

1. Money can buy happiness up to about $75,000—after that, it has no significant effect on your emotional well-being, according to research in the U.S.
2. Happiness is primarily the result of day-to-day living experiences.
3. Trying too hard to be happy can lead to selfishness.
4. Spending more time with family and friends is an effective way to find happiness.
5. Pursuing vague happiness goals may be more effective than setting specific goals.
6. Your own individual happiness may spread happiness to other people in your community.
7. Your individual happiness may improve your job performance or lead to a better job.
8. Participating in spiritual activities raises your happiness and correlates with your providing emotional support to others, making them happy in turn.[178]

Because happiness is primarily the result of one's day-to-day living experience, *where* you live makes a critical difference in your perception of happiness. These are the happiest cities on the planet, according to the 2020 World Happiness Report:

PERCEIVED HAPPINESS BY CITY[179]	
1. Helsinki, Finland	6. Bergen, Norway
2. Aarhus, Denmark	7. Oslo, Norway
3. Wellington, New Zealand	8. Tel Aviv, Israel
4. Zurich, Switzerland	9. Stockholm, Sweden
5. Copenhagen, Denmark	10. Brisbane, Australia

You may have noticed that the United States didn't make it into the top 10. America's happiest city came in at number 18.

What happy cities have in common. The happiest cities share three features: low corruption rates, universal public services, and great access to the outdoors. The one that surprised me the most is "access to the outdoors."

According to Alliance Visa Ltd, "If you ask a Scandinavian what makes them so happy to be living in their country, most will reply that they feel secure, all their basic needs are met and they don't have to fear being broke. They have very little to stress about since their social programs provide so much support. Everyone has a chance at achieving higher education whereas in countries like the USA and the UK those who come from low-income households struggle to afford university and tend to turn to work at low minimum wage paid jobs to get by. Being outdoors is a great national pastime for Scandinavians, everyone goes for long walks regardless of the weather."[140]

HAPPINESS AND HOUSING

Everyone needs a place to live, and they are willing to pay more for nice surroundings than for dismal surroundings. The Cambridge Dictionary defines beauty "as the quality of being pleasing, especially to look at, or someone or something that gives great pleasure, especially when you look at it." We are all keenly aware that people in general know the difference between the beautiful side of the tracks and the unattractive side of the tracks, even though some idealists and dreamers tell us otherwise.

Beauty attracts. Real estate agents know that buyers look for beauty—specimen trees, lush shrubbery, flower beds, narrow streets, wide sidewalks, vernacular architecture, small unlit signage, walking paths, riverside parks, street furniture, free flowing streams, fish ponds, songbirds, quiet, and clean air.

Ugly repels. Real estate agents also know that buyers are repelled by ugly—concrete, chain-link fencing, razor wire, modern architecture, graffiti, trash, wide streets, narrow sidewalks, large light up signs, minimal greenery, channelized streams, glaring lights, strip malls, noise, and smog.

So housing is very much a part of human happiness. The poor segregated into ugly and dilapidated housing are very much damaged by living where the more fortunate can afford not to live because they too know the difference between the beautiful and the ugly—and they don't like ugly any more than do the higher classes.

So, since the 1880s, American trend setters and government leaders have done their best to improve the aesthetic quality of housing for all Americans, even during economic recessions and two World Wars.

City Beautiful movement. The City Beautiful Movement was a reform philosophy of North American architecture and urban planning that was prominent during the 1890s and 1900s. City Beautiful was part of a larger progressive social reform movement led by the upper-middle class who were appalled by the poverty-stricken living conditions in America's biggest cities. City Beautiful advocates believed beautification would lead to better living accommodations, better health and a better quality of life for the lower classes.[141]

Depression-era housing. In 1929, with the onset of the Great Depression, the building of new homes nearly halted, repairs went unfinished, and slums expanded. Additionally, thousands of home-owners were unable to make payments on their mortgages. By 1933, nearly half of all home mortgages were in default. The home financing system was sliding toward complete collapse. Recovery didn't come until the Second World War ended.

Post-WWII housing. Post-WWII housing lasted from 1945 until around 1960. William and Alfred Levitt won a wartime contract to construct mass-produced military homes in Norfolk, Virginia. When the war ended, the Levitt brothers used their wartime experience to provide affordable housing in the suburbs—Cape Cod–style, a living room with fireplace, two bedrooms, and one bath—approximately 750 square feet—small by today's standards, but adequate at the time. Many of the prospective homebuyers qualified for GI Bill of Rights home loans.

The Levitt brothers owned timber and a sawmill, made their own nails and cement, and prefabricated structures using jigs and templates. They purchased appliances directly from manufacturers. They developed a system whereby home production was broken into 27 steps, allowing the Levitt brothers to construct a home in minutes.

Builders from coast-to-coast emulated the Levitt brothers, building oodles of bare-bones homes—concrete slab, three bedrooms, one bath, wall heater in the hall, washer hookup in the one-car garage, and one spindly tree in the front yard. Eventually supply caught up with demand, so around 1960 home construction drastically improved: central heating, whole-house insulation, family rooms, two-car garages, washer and dryer hookups inside the home—and one-spindly tree in the front yard.

Along came the McMansions. "Beginning in California in the 1980s, the larger home concept was intended to fill a gap between the more modest suburban tract housing and the upscale custom homes found in gated, waterfront, or golf course communities. . . . McMansions often mix a variety of architectural styles and elements, combining quoins, steeply sloped roofs, multiple roof lines, complicated massing and pronounced dormers, all producing what some consider an unpleasant jumbled appearance."[142]

Doubling up—a step back. According to newly released Census Bureau data, there has been a steady decrease in the size of the average

U.S. household over time, from 5.79 people per household in 1790 to 2.58 in 2010. But people per household increased in 2018 to 2.63 people.

The increase in household size since the Great Recession, has come about because more Americans are sharing living quarters. In 2019, 20 percent of households shared households, up from 17 percent in 2007.

The increase in household size is significant because rising household size reduces the demand for housing, resulting in less residential construction and less demand for home appliances and furniture.

The increase in household size also hides a lot of poverty because doubling up raises household income as measured by the U. S. Census Bureau.

Rising household size is a clear indicator that the economy is performing poorly, not an indicator of good times ahead.[143]

Average home size—risky behavior. In 1973, the median new single-family home had 1,525 square feet. By 2018, it had grown to 2,435 square feet. During this same time frame, American "must haves" changed: basement guest suites are no longer rare; many homeowners want a home office; the master suite has become cavernous; walk-in closets might be bigger than the bedroom you had as a child; and it's not a master suite without its own adjoining bathroom. Add to this extravagance man caves, she sheds, and bonus rooms.

Between 1973 and 2018, incomes rose about 600 percent in the U.S., but home prices rose by more than 900 percent. Americans can't seem to control their wants.[144]

Average home cost—more risky behavior. Laura Mueller, of Move, Inc. warns us that everything is bigger when you buy a bigger home. "It's not just your monthly premium that's going to rise. Buying a bigger home means:

- Higher closing costs
- Higher furnishing costs
- Higher property taxes
- Higher homeowner's insurance costs
- Higher utility costs
- Higher repair and maintenance costs
- Higher energy costs
- Higher renovation costs

All of these costs add up fast—you need to think about your financial future."[145]

Low-income housing—still expensive. According to the 2017 Construction Cost survey by the National Association of Home Builders, the average cost to build a home in this country is $154 per square foot.[146] On average, it will cost you:

$154,000 to build 1,000-square-feet

$231,000 to build 1,500-square-feet

$308,000 to build 2,000-square-feet

Housing—don't overspend. Don't overextend yourself by buying more house than you can afford. People who buy too much house often find that they can't make their mortgage payments when an emergency strikes—medical bills, reduced income, unexpected emergency. Play it safe buy within your means. Below is approximately how much income a family needs to own a modest 1,000 square foot home:

- Purchase Price: $154,000
- Down Payment: $0
- Interest Rate: 3.75%
- Term of Loan: 30 years
- Percent of Income: 28

To afford a home that costs $154,000 with a down payment of $0, you'd need to earn $30,566 per year before tax. The monthly payment on the home would be $713 before tax.[147] $30,566 per year is $14.69 an hour—don't keep marching around in the streets asking for a $15 an hour minimum wage, you should be asking for a $20 per hour minimum wage—or more.

"Brother, can you spare a dime?"[148] The root cause of the affordable housing crisis is insufficient income. For Americans with a high school education or less, wages have been going down for more than 40 years. That's why they can't afford to buy market-rate homes or pay market-rate rent anywhere in America.

The solution is not all that mystifying: raise wages. Currently, the federal minimum wage is $7.25 per hour, not enough to make ends meet no matter where you live. According to Enterprise Community Partners, Inc:

- "A household earning minimum wage cannot afford a modest rental anywhere in the U.S.," and "As of 2009, there was a 5.5 million shortfall in affordable housing units compared to the poor renters who need them."[149]
- "The National Employment Law Project released an exhaustive report in 2016 looking at every federal minimum wage hike since 1938. The investigators found that year-over-year employment increased 68 percent of the time after each wage hike. What's more, the industries most affected by minimum wage more often saw jumps in employment: 73 percent of the time in retail and 82 percent in leisure and hospitality."

REAL AVERAGE HOURLY WAGE, BY EDUCATION, 1979–2017, IN 2012 US DOLLARS[150]				
	< High School	High School	College Degree	Advanced Degree
1979	$14.85	$16.67	$23.36	$28.53
2017	$13.90	$17.85	$32.49	$41.36

If your wages stagnate or keep going down year after year, you're not likely to buy a home or a car or much of anything else. As just one example of wage disparity, *CNN Business* reported in 2018 that "Walmart's CEO makes a lot more than the company's median worker. 1,188 times more, to be exact. Doug McMillon earned $22.8 million during the retailer's last fiscal year . . . according to a company filing. Walmart's median employee, meanwhile, earned $19,177 in the same period. The retailer, which is the nation's largest private-sector employer, has about 2.3 million global employees, including full-time and part-time workers. Roughly 1.5 million are in the United States."[151]

Housing and city planning. Planning literature is filled with schemes to solve the low-income housing crisis by building subsidized housing for the poor, cutting up single-family housing into low rent apartments, and increasing housing density and eliminating car parking.

But none of these schemes address the root cause of homelessness and doubling up: maldistribution of wealth—insufficient incomes.

Avoiding the root cause. In 2013 the Public Broadcasting Service (PBS) ran a wonderful documentary series called *The African Americans: Many Rivers to Cross*, presented by Harvard scholar Henry Louis Gates, Jr. One episode explained how the American government spent 300 years trying to find effective ways to deal with runaway slaves rather than freeing them and thus eliminating the root cause of running.[152] Now the American government is trying to find effective ways to deal with low-income housing rather than raising incomes, thus eliminating the root cause. The government is still trying to find effective ways to deal with symptoms rather than trying to eliminate the root cause—low wages.

"In January of 2018 the federal government statistics gave comprehensive encompassing nationwide statistics, with a total number of 552,830 [homeless] individuals."[153]

When I worked as an Alinsky Organizer in the San Francisco area, many of the people I worked with were homeless or living in slums. I quickly learned that to help the poor, my organization—United Progresso Arriva (UPA)—needed to sort people into three groups:

- Unemployed, looking for work—find them a job.
- Underpaid, living on minimum wage—get them better pay.
- Mentally ill, with disrupted thinking—get them treatment.

Those who wanted to help—social workers, counselors, church groups, busybodies—had never heard of these three categories. So, over the years, time and time again, they have failed to solve homelessness; they have offered unneeded treatments to the unemployed and tried to find jobs for the dysfunctional mentally ill. The people in my organization (UPA) knew who was out of money and who was out of their mind. The do-gooders didn't seem to be able to figure it out.

So over and over again we watched subsidized housing being handed out to dysfunctional families who trashed every house they were given, leaving behind rats, roaches, filth, and holes punched in the walls. Normal people who were cash poor waited for housing that never came. Social workers seem to be the easiest people in the world to con—and the mentally ill know just how to con them.

As an Alinsky Organizer I lived with other members of my organization in the same slums as those we were attempting to help (in the social sciences that's called being a participant observer). Over several years, I guided UPA to take responsibility for community improvement.

They obtained grants for housing rehabilitation, opened a senior citizen center, sponsored a youth center, operated a Head Start program, ran a buyer's cooperative, initiated low-income housing construction, and operated their own Section 8 housing agency. They also obtained a HUD grant to construct Wesley Manor, a 156-unit high-rise residential building. UPA also came across a 40-building slum apartment block scheduled for demolition. UPA urged tenants to fight back against eviction and withhold their rent for six-months. In the end, the city forced the slum landlord to rehabilitate all 40 buildings and to charge fair rents. Some 50-years later, the housing block is still in good repair and considered to be a desirable place to live.

When I hear about grand plans to solve the low-income housing shortfall, I always ask, "Where are the results on the land?" The government has been making up excuses for inaction for the past 40 years, and I'm tired of the malarkey.

Are we happy? Economists John Helliwell, Richard Layard, and Jeffrey Sachs evaluated 156 countries by their happiness levels. Their study measured six metrics to develop their rankings—freedom, generosity, income, trust, healthy life expectancy, and social support:

"The U.S. ranks at No. 19 in the 2019 report . . . . America ranked 12th for generosity, 37th for social support and 42nd for corruption. In addition, the United States placed 61st in terms of freedom."[154]

Unhappiness—root cause. Americans are not very happy, and the root cause of much unhappiness is our lack of affordable health care. One of the largest drivers of happiness according to the annual General Social Survey conducted by the University of Chicago, is health care that has become more expensive and less available. Additionally, the United States is in the longest decline in life expectancy since World War I, caused by rising suicides and drug overdoses, even though we are in one of the longest economic expansions ever.[155]

America is the only rich country without universal health care.

9. SEVEN-GENERATION SUSTAINABILITY CITY WIDE

According to the philosophy of the Iroquois Confederacy, "we must consider the impact of our decisions on the next seven generations."[156]

But the bible calls upon us to go even further. The Jewish Bible tells us that the creator's long run expectation is that we will exercise responsible stewardship over the earth until the end of time—and that expectation is found in Genesis 1:26

Looking for guidance, I copied the following version of Genesis 1:26 from Mechon Mamre, a small group of observant Jewish Torah scholars in Israel:

"And God said: "Let us make man in our image, after our likeness; and let them have dominion over the fish of the sea, and over the fowl of the air, and over the cattle, and over all the earth, and over every creeping thing that creepeth upon the earth."[157]

Then, looking for a simpler explanation that I could easily understand, I turned to American Biblical scholars who write in America's everyday language.

Philip C. L. Gray, Vice President of Catholics United for the

Faith, writing in *Lay Witness*, says: "While some may consider the term 'dominion' in this passage to be the only direct reference to 'stewardship,' the entire passage reveals that the stewardship expected of Adam and Eve and all of us has three essential characteristics. It is collective; it respects the purpose for which things exist; and it respects the dignity of each person.[158]

Along the same line of thought, the Church of Jesus Christ of Latter-day Saints, tells us "The earth and all things on it should be used responsibly to sustain the human family. However, all are stewards — not owners — over this earth and its bounty and will be accountable before God for what they do with His creations."[159]

After reading Genesis 1:26, and the religious thought behind it, I've come to the conclusion that America has lost its respect of the purpose for which things exist, and its respect for the dignity of each person—a loss of respect that could eventually lead to the downfall of our nation.

David Rhoads, writing in *Lutherans Restoring Creation*, has this to say: "In our Christian life, the key to making our world sustainable is viewing our change of behavior and our sacrifices as acts of love and kindness toward all creation—toward other people; toward other creatures; and toward the well-being of land, sea, and air."

So, seven-generation sustainability appears to be only the short-term directive. Genesis explains the long-term directive: We must live by acts of love and kindness toward all creation.

Chapter 3
THE LIMITED PLAN

A limited or intermediate plan applies to a smaller land area than the general plan and contains more detail. It may cover a shorter time frame and focus on a more specific goal. For continuity's sake, I'll address the same aspects as I did for the general plan—the five physical development aspects taken from the City Planning Primer and the four intangible aspects that I added to bring city planning into the twenty-first century: basic human needs, quality of life, happiness and seven-generation sustainability.

This second-level plan supports the first-level general plan by concentrating on a distinct land area or government function, such as the siting of police substations, firehouses, parks and playgrounds, or underground utilities. It is common for a city to have several limited plans.

1. ECONOMIC TREND—LIMITED PLANS

The job of the local planning authority is to guide the economic evolution of the city rather than stand by and watch low quality design and construction, poor siting of businesses, and inappropriate landscape architecture dissipate the sense of place and lead to economic decline.

Which of the nine nations are you in? These days it can be hard to tell which of the Nine Nations of North America you're in, because so much of America has been subjected to look-alike real estate development, mass-produced imported products, and chain restaurant quasi-food. America has given away its local stores, local factories, and local food in exchange for cultural impoverishment and declining quality of life. About all that's left to enjoy is *Diners, Drive-Ins and Dives*—Guy Fieri traveling the nation on the Food Network for a real-deal taste of home.[160]

When was your city founded? That may be hard to see, because the 150-year-old stores on Main Street may have been concealed behind turquoise and aluminum false fronts or torn down and replaced by cement block and pre-engineered metal buildings. And about the same goes for culturally significant houses—now clad in aluminum siding. My neighboring town in Arizona, Peoria, founded in 1897, was bulldozed to make way for progress. Now the original townsite is nothing more than a closed-down regional mall, abandoned big-box retail buildings, and fields of weeds. A lack of foresight (city planning) has turned the local American dream into an American nightmare. The only reason I ever go to downtown Peoria is to buy treats from K-May Donuts and Bagels—they're the best.

BRAINSTORMING

System-built modular homes are built to the International Residential Code to comply with state and municipal building codes for residential construction. They can look like homes from any historical period. Three popular styles that can be easily reproduced are the Bungalow, 1900–1940; Arts and Crafts, 1870–1920; and the American Foursquare, 1890–1930. Fortunately, most older neighborhoods were divided into smaller lots that are just the right size for period reproductions and infill housing. Residents feel better about their surroundings when houses complement each other without being boring look-alikes.

What's the historic growth curve for your city? The growth of a city is nearly identical to the growth of a business: development; start-up; growth; expansion; maturity. But even after your city reaches maturity, it needs to set a new course of action: creating grandeur. If your city fails to become an attraction—like Paris, London, or Rome— you are most likely going to go into decline at some point in the future. Once a city goes into decline, it is very difficult and expensive to revive it. Usually, people find it easier to just move away.

BRAINSTORMING

Many declining cities look bad. When I drive through a declining city, I look for signs of deferred maintenance. To bring your city back from the dead, you have to eliminate unsightly properties by enforcing your local ordinances. It's not easy.

- **Yard maintenance.** Private land, including alleys or easements, must be free of unsightly conditions.
- **Graffiti.** Graffiti located on private property must be removed.
- **Illegal signs.** Permanent sign structures must have valid permits or be removed.
- **Accumulation of debris.** Property must be kept free of garbage or litter.
- **Building exterior.** Properties must be maintained in good condition—free of peeling paint, broken fences, or deteriorating roofs.
- **Vehicles.** Abandoned or junk vehicles, or vehicles being repaired, need to be stored in fully enclosed, non-visible locations.

Enforcing local ordinances is an essential part of city planning, it is how cities prevent neighborhoods from becoming slums.

Growth over the next 20 years. People like to think that their city will grow at a predictable rate, but it won't. Cities may stop growing for any number of reasons. But the end of growth needn't lead to a decline in the value of your city. It may even be an opportunity to grow *better*. Statistically many people say they want to live is smaller, quieter communities—many quieter places are learning how to attract new residents who want to get away from fast paced, ever changing growth centers—stability can be very comforting.

BRAINSTORMING

Joel Garreau, in his 1991 book *Edge City: Life on the New Frontier,* argued that the "edge city" had become the standard form of urban growth worldwide. But today Garreau, takes the position that because of technological change, the edge city may be losing out to a new phenomenon—small beautiful cities:

> "Now that white-collar workers can work from anywhere, [Garreau] believes, more of them are moving to places where they may have previously just vacationed—but which hold enough people like themselves that they can still enjoy face-to-face contact with others in their field. Small, beautiful cities that foster the arts and human engagement are the future."[161]

Now that Covid-19 has taught people that they can work from home, I suspect that many of them have started thinking about how they can keep their jobs and move to Bedford Falls, Cabot Cove, Hope Valley, Lake Wobegon, or Toon Town.

WHAT IS URBAN SPRAWL

Sprawl is a mindset, not an inevitability. Arizona, where I now live, is the wild west of real estate development. It doesn't care about quality of life as much as it cares about more taxes for the city. Anything goes. I recently drove past a new real estate development that was disgusting to me—a slum before it was even occupied. I mentioned it to a few friends, who just shrugged their shoulders and said, "What did you expect in a city that never says no to a real estate developer?" In the long run, issuing haphazard planning permits will come back to bite, but by then the local public officials will have moseyed along to the next watering hole.

Sprawl—common definition. Sprawl is defined as "to spread or develop irregularly or without restraint." The key words are "without restraint." Sprawl is also the unrestricted spread of housing, commerce, and roads over a large expanse of land, with little concern for urban planning or regard for who will pay for infrastructure to service new development. The cost of providing infrastructure is rarely recouped through property taxes, amounting to a huge subsidy for real estate developers and the new residents, at the expense of other taxpayers.

Sprawl—my own definition. I'm not opposed to low density single-family housing, so I define urban sprawl differently:

- Urban sprawl is not low-density urbanization. It's unruly urbanization.
- Urban sprawl is development of Class I to Class IV fertile agricultural land, wetland ecosystems, floodplains, critical habitat and the like.

Your local plans can put a stop to urban sprawl by excluding primordial places, performing cost-benefit analyses, and selecting a path of growth that urbanizes what the Cambridge dictionary calls "land that is found on the edge of cultivated areas and is often difficult to grow crops on."

In regard to urban sprawl, Genesis 1:26 tells us to—respect the purpose for which things exist.

BRAINSTORMING

Emerging infrastructure technology. Installing infrastructure such as underground utilities, is a major capital expense. Fortunately, there are some new ways to upgrade your infrastructure. Trenchless construction methods, for example, are generally more cost-effective than traditional methods. Trenchless construction includes tunneling, horizontal directional drilling, pipe ramming, pipe jacking, and other ways to underground pipelines and cables with minimal excavation. Trenchless rehabilitation includes sliplining, thermoformed pipe, shotcrete, gunite, cured-in-place pipe, and other ways to replace worn-out buried pipes without excavation.[162]

A California company, TechniSoil Industrial, has devised a process that integrates recycled plastic into road repaving. The process involves a chain of vehicles that scoop up the top three inches of asphalt, which is then ground on a mill and mixed with a binder of up to 20 percent liquid plastic. The blend is deposited back on the road and rolled. No heat is involved.[163]

Stop doing things the old way. Move on to state-of-the-art procedures and processes—even if it means disposing of still-usable equipment and retraining city crews. A lot of people are resistant to change, though, even when it is for the common good.

Preserve local history. Many Americans, especially preservationists, can't cope with the concept of continuity preservation. In America, if a historic building or place is lost to fire, flood, rot, or deliberate intent, it is considered lost forever. In Europe, because of its history of warfare, people are accustomed to periodic rebuilding. Many of the "ancient cities of Europe" that Americans go all the way across the Atlantic Ocean to photograph were actually built from scratch after the Second World War.

As an example, Italy's Montecasino Monastery was founded by St. Benedict in about 529 A.D. Around 577, the monastery was destroyed by invading Lombards. Then in 883 the Saracens sacked the monastery and burned it down. A third destruction was caused by an earthquake in 1349. Each time, though, the monastery was reconstructed, becoming bigger and more imposing in its appearance.[164] Then on February 15, 1944, a WWII army officer, translating an intercepted radio message, mistook the German word for "abbot" for a similar word meaning "battalion." Within three hours, Montecasino was reduced to rubble.[165] After the war ended, the monks spent ten years reconstructing it.

In America, historic preservation purists likely would have insisted that Montecasino be replaced by a commemorative plaque. The National Park Service Technical Preservation Services says, "Because of the potential for historical error in the absence of sound physical evidence, this treatment can be justified only rarely. . . . Reconstructing a historic building should only be considered when there is accurate documentation on which to base it. [T]he reconstructed building must be clearly identified as a contemporary recreation."[166]

I've driven all over Europe and don't recall seeing signs saying "contemporary recreation"—not anywhere, not on Cologne Cathedral, not on Konigsberg Cathedral, and not on Warsaw's Royal Castle and the 85 percent of Warsaw that was destroyed by the Nazis during the Second World War.

BRAINSTORMING

Think of your city as a movie set. Anything can be changed to look the way you want it to look. Downtown Paso Robles, California, is being moved back in time to a more picturesque period, one building at a time, slowly enough that tourists don't notice that neon, plastic, and the 1950s are fading away. They are being replaced with the "wine country milieu" they forgot to build way back when.

2. TRANSPORTATION—LIMITED PLANS

Three factors must be taken into consideration when discussing transportation:

- **Distance is measured in time.** The trip on the magnetic levitation train running the nineteen miles between Shanghai Hongqiao International Airport and the city takes 15 minutes. The trip by car driving the 3 miles between Boston's Logan International Airport and the city takes 17 minutes—and wait 'til you see the parking rates.

- **The journey is point-to-point or pick-up-and-drop-off.** Donkey cart, stagecoach, bus, and streetcar take passengers from point to point—and the bus won't stop at the Starbucks drive-up window so you can get a latte. Walking, riding a horse, cycling, and skateboarding start where you are and take you where you want to be—and you can always tie up your horse at the Starbucks hitching post.

- **Travel is done as a group or individually.** Traveling in a group means you get to sit next to those who don't bathe and may babble incoherently, depart with your laptop, and give you Covid-19. And what are you going to do with your children, pets, and grocery bags? Travelling individually means you can talk on your cell phone, sing out loud, eat fast food, and drink coffee. You can also pack your laptop and carry all your personal stuff around with you—and still have room for the kids and pets.

Major thoroughfares. In 1928 planners used the term "thoroughfare" to describe a major roadway. Today a thoroughfare would be referred to as an "arterial roadway." Since the end of the Second World War and the rise of the curvilinear street pattern, planners have formalized the hierarchy of roadways, giving them these names: local, collector, arterial, expressway, and freeway.

At the time of the Roman Empire, an arterial was a 40-foot-wide *decumanus*, a collector was a 20-foot-wide *cardo*, and a local was a 15-foot-wide *vicinae*. Americans aren't the first people to come up with differentiated roadways.

Older American cities west of New England are generally laid out in a gridiron pattern based on the Public Land Survey System. Under this system, land was subdivided into squares of decreasing size, and country roadways were spaced half a mile apart. Fortuitously, dividing the land into squares and spacing roads this way created a convenient roadway pattern for an urban area—the gridiron. The gridiron pattern led to the now-familiar lot and block layouts we see in most nineteenth-century cities. Rectangular blocks and lots originally faced identical roadways of equal width, laced together in an interconnected grid. Later on, roadways at half-mile intervals were widened to accommodate fast-moving traffic, and that fast-moving traffic was forbidden to use the narrower, quieter streets. This was done to protect children from fast horses. (As a child growing up in Newcastle upon Tyne, my mother barely survived an encounter with a runaway coal wagon.)

Many city planners believe that America should return to the gridiron pattern as a way of increasing urban population density and encouraging walking. But other city planners argue the opposite—and neither side will ever concede. But in most cities, planners are stuck with the existing street pattern—planners have to work with what they have inherited.

BRAINSTORMING

Whichever roadway pattern your city presently has it will probably continue into the future unchanged. But that doesn't mean that pattern can't be improved. Just don't fall for quirky roadway patterns:

- Don't lay out roadways in concentric circles as in Sun City, Arizona, where we now live. It makes both driving and walking nearly impossible. When we get out-of-town visitors, we have to meet them out on the state highway and guide them to our home.

- Don't let a sick mind talk you into building a freeway through your city. A freeway is for cross-country driving, not shuttling around town. From decades of driving around the Los Angeles basin, I learned to use surface roadways—they're much faster.

Back around 1965, California came up with an alternative approach to the major thoroughfare: the expressway. California defines an expressway as "an arterial highway for through traffic which may have partial control of access, but which may or may not be divided or have grade separations at intersections."[167] In Northern California, for instance, Santa Clara County built a 377-mile expressway network of extra-wide streets to haul commuters from [San Jose's Almaden Valley to Milpitas and Palo Alto. Access points are a mile or two apart at arterial street intersections. Most expressways have a landscaped median strip and three lanes of traffic going in each direction. There are few grade separations and only infrequent curb cuts that allow access to major employment or shopping centers.

Speed limits are usually 45 mph, though actual average travel times are about the same as on freeways. Expressways solve a lot of transportation problems—and they look good, with their lavish landscaping. But of course, transportation engineers keep trying to convert expressways into freeways.

The Green Book—command-and-control. The Federal Highway Administration's "Green Book" consists of transportation standards that perpetuate mid-twentieth-century transportation philosophy. The Green Book makes "it difficult for cities to design streets that improve pedestrian and bicyclist safety at the expense of vehicle throughput," according to a report prepared by the Center for Law, Energy, and the Environment at the Berkeley Law School.[168]

Command-and-control: Fresno, California. According to John Urgo, Meredith Wilensky, and Steven Weissman, "For the last 40 years, Fresno has required residential streets to have a right of way that is at least 40 feet wide, while arterial streets have a minimum width of 106 feet."[169] I know from my eight years of teaching school in Fresno that walking (actually running) across a 106-foot street is death-defying. (I rode the bus to my school, and the bus stop was on the far side of a fast-moving arterial. Yes, I rode the bus. That's why I know about bus commuting.)

Defying command-and-control: Oregon. According to a report written by Oregon's Neighborhood Streets Project Stakeholders, the State of Oregon has found that "deaths and injuries to pedestrians increase significantly as the speed of motor vehicles goes up. A typical 36-foot-wide residential street has 1.21 collisions/mile/year as opposed to 0.32 for a 24-foot-wide street. The safest streets were narrow, slow, 24-foot-wide streets."[170] Since the year 2000, Oregon has been reducing the width of streets to promote safety and encourage peace and quiet in residential neighborhoods.

Defying command-and-control: San Pablo, California. One

of the first communities I worked in as a planner had very narrow streets—24 feet. The city was conveniently walkable. And by using only 18 percent of the land for streets, housing density soared to 25 units per acre—extremely high density for a quiet community of mostly single-family homes. San Pablo is a walkable city.

Defying common sense: Sun City, Arizona. Out in the desert where I live now, the local streets are 32 feet wide—16 feet wider than needed. Only a few cars drive by our home in a day, nearly all of them neighbors' cars. All we need is one driving lane and one combined driving and parking lane—homeowners don't park their cars on the streets in Sun City. (We're afraid our cars will melt when the temperature gets up around 120 degrees.) All the excess pavement does is use up land and encourage speeding.

Street railways. Trolleys or streetcars, now puffed up and rechristened "light rail," are remnants from the past—not the wave of the future.

Transit busses. We lived in Palm Springs, California, for a number of years. But because both of us have spinal cord damage, we had to arrange for medical transportation on a regular basis to Rancho Los Amigos National Rehabilitation Center 100 miles away in Downey, California. The trip on Interstate 10 takes three hours, or sometimes a lot longer. For several years we shuttled back and forth, staying in hotels and eating restaurant food. Then our favorite doctor transferred to Arizona—so we followed.

Our Arizona home is within 2.1 miles of the hospital—close enough to wheel there in a motor-assisted chair, a 45-minute trip. But it's also 2 miles from the nearest shopping, 2 miles from physical therapy, and 2 miles from the podiatrist. Everything we need is at least

2 miles away—even the bus stop. The buses line up on the dead-end street between the podiatrist's office and the physical therapy clinic.

Riding the bus is obviously impractical where we live, so buses drive around empty most of the day, carrying only one or two passengers during peak hours. I often wonder if the federal government pays the county to run this highly subsidized bus service to demonstrate how wonderful life will be after city planners have forced us to give up our politically incorrect private cars. Nor are we going to give up our single-family home, our tree-filled garden (more than 40 trees), or our access to nine golf courses and nine recreation centers (swimming, weights, saunas, bowling, tennis, hobbies, crafts, massages, restaurants, etc.) so we can live downtown in a Brutalist-style high-rise condominium on a bus route.

On the other hand, I lived in the San Francisco Bay Area for many years and often rode public transportation. But San Francisco is the second-most densely populated city in America. Even as a child I thought nothing of jumping on and off cable cars or riding streetcars. Later on, living in Berkeley, I regularly rode, Bay Area Rapid Transit (BART) under the bay, then transferred to the North Judah street car line that went all the way west to the Pacific Ocean. It was fast and cheap—whereas parking a car in Berkeley and San Francisco can be impossible.

Yet even in overcrowded San Francisco, people own cars. Cars represent independence and autonomy—the bus isn't going to take you on a leisurely drive through wine country on the weekend—cars aren't just used for commuting to work.

VEHICLE AVAILABILITY IN SAN FRANCISCO, 2000		
Vehicles available	Households	Percent
Total Households	325,596	
None	11,982	10.3
One	48,138	41.2
Two	41,434	35.5
Three	11,051	9.5
Four	3,242	2.8
Five or more	877	0.8
Sum		100.1

BRAINSTORMING

Your city already exists, and it isn't going to evolve very quickly, so, your local planning authority has to adjust bus lines and other forms of rapid transit to reflect the existing reality. Local plans need to pass the reasonable person test. According to the *Merriam-Webster Dictionary of Law*, the legal definition of "reasonable person" is "a fictional person with an ordinary degree of reason, prudence, care, foresight, or intelligence whose conduct, conclusion, or expectation in relation to a particular circumstance or fact is used as an objective standard by which to measure or determine something."[171]

You have to figure out what will work in your city and what won't. Otherwise, you'll end up trying to put a square peg in a round hole.

Transportation—freight railways. A tractor-pulled semitrailer or "dry van" carries as much as 52,000 pounds of cargo. A railroad freight car carries as much as 250,000 pounds.[213] Many freight trains pull 110 freight cars that carry two piggyback dry vans each. That eliminates 220 over-the-road truck drivers. And now the single locomotive engineer is being replaced by a robot.

Since the Second World War, many small towns have lost their freight trains in the name of progress. The consequence has been costly to the nation and a disaster for small towns. Now that the next-generation trains are designed with self-propelled rail cars and robot engineers, this would be a good time to explore the possibility of restoring rail freight service.

Transportation—waterways and harbors. A standard-size barge operating on a major river carries three million pounds. Barges are normally tied together into 15 barge "tows." [214] Many people in rural Alaska have a year's worth of food, clothing, and household goods delivered by barge each spring. Expediters in Seattle provide grocery lists and know how to pack the shipping containers so items are available during the month they are needed. It takes a while to learn what to buy for a whole year, but in the long run it's quite convenient.

Many American cities have allowed their canals, harbors, and barge traffic to die off in favor of truck delivery. That has turned out to be shortsighted. Does your city have the wherewithal to bring back cost-effective barge traffic?

Transportation—public utilities. Overhead power lines are typically more economical than underground power lines. But they are susceptible to damage from wind-borne tree branches, debris, high winds, and ice-loading conditions from extreme weather. Such damage can cause power outages that cannot be restored for days or weeks, and repair costs can be in the billions of dollars. During long outages, there are also intangible impacts, such as despair, discomfort, anxiety and helplessness. Furthermore, there are direct economic losses caused by lost economic activity, from food spoilage to looting.

Whenever a major weather-related catastrophe occurs, people ask, "Why can't overhead power lines be undergrounded?" The answer is that they can, but it's expensive.

According to Wisconsin's Public Service Commission, the cost of constructing underground transmission lines is four to fourteen times more expensive than installing comparable overhead lines. Trenching through the earth along the entire line route is the biggest cost. In one neighborhood in Orlando, Florida, for example, a homebuyer must pay an additional $15,000 for underground power service.[172] Back a half-century ago, when I was in planning school, I was told that public utility providers were going to set aside enough money each year to systematically underground old and obsolete overhead utility lines—but it never happened. It got in the way of quarterly profits. Undergrounding utility lines is a quality-of-life issue. In this case, America's quality of life is going down, not up.

But the time is approaching when both customers and government will demand undergrounding of overhead wiring. The change will be precipitated by all-too-frequent power outages caused by natural disasters—outages that lower the quality of life, disrupt commerce, and seem to occur more and more frequently.[173] Undergrounding gives your city a clean look that makes people feel good and gives their eyes a break.

3. RECREATION—LIMITED PLANS

Joe McCarthy, writing for *Global Citizen*, asks this question: So, what makes a good public park? The following is an abbreviated version of McCarthy's list:

- **Central location.** Your local park needs to be accessible to all social classes. There should be a park within walking distance of your home (about half a mile, or a walk of 10 to 30 minutes).
- **Lots of vegetation.** Your local park needs to have many trees and at least one pond as a focal point, and it should have lots of grass to sit and walk on.
- **Wildlife and birds.** There should be habitat for small animals and birds. Landscaping should provide food and shelter for many species—the park should look like a natural woodland.

- **Safety.** Your local park needs to feel like a sanctuary, and it needs to have a well-marked safe place where a threatened person can be seen and heard by security and where a lost child can go to seek help.
- **Walking paths.** Your local park needs lots of meandering walking paths, plus benches where walkers can rest.
- **Cultural events.** Your local park needs to be a place for gathering and celebrating. A bandstand or picnic pod will do.[215]

Playgrounds. Play areas are essential. One company that builds playgrounds, Landscape Structures, says, "We're dedicated researchers, educators, and experts passionate about creating innovative playground designs that help children grow up healthy and happy."[174] There's no excuse for your city not to have well-equipped and conveniently located playgrounds. Contact a professional playground designer and do some planning. And don't forget to plant some shade trees!

Linear parks. A linear park or trail is far better than a regular park. That's another reason for having a river run through your city: it provides a perfect setting for a linear park. Linear parks can serve as walking or bicycling routes for those who commute to work. They open up your city, giving it a feeling of freedom from the confines of roadways and blocks of buildings. And they create value by increasing the value of surrounding taxable land.

In some places linear parks have been created from abandoned railroad rights of way, and in other places from underground utility easements. Planning from scratch, your city should preplan linear parks for land areas that have not yet been developed. Redevelopment project areas may also be replatted to create linear parks.

BRAINSTORMING

Most city parks I'm familiar with are "over-tended"—maintained by lawnmower jockeys who don't understand plant growth. By over tending, I mean cutting grass too short, topping trees and turning shrubs into lollypops and boxes with hedge shears. Lawnmower jockeys also take all of the clippings to the dump instead of returning them to the soil as mulch.

Parks should look a little rustic, plants should be allowed to grow to their mature height and spread. People who know landscaping can spot the difference, just by driving by a park.

4. PUBLIC FACILITIES—LIMITED PLANS

Public buildings should incorporate the indigenous architectural style of your "nation". Local climate also determines your architectural style. That is why you need to discourage architectural styles from other places.

Writes Lucia in *Modlar*, "A desert environment is hostile by nature; building in the desert means having to prepare your design to withstand extreme sunlight and heat, and relentless cold temperatures—all in one day."[175] Where I live out in the desert, summer temperatures are usually around 110°F, so buildings need to provide shade and shelter from the heat. I've landscaped my yard with plants that shade my home and lower the exterior wall temperature by 15°F.

Driving my politically incorrect car from one city hall to another within the Phoenix Metropolitan Area, what I see is America's nationwide shopping mall cartoon architecture applied to civic buildings. The results are vile. But then, I don't know if these architects learned their craft at Wurster Hall, home to UC Berkeley's architecture department. Wurster Hall "is often voted Berkeley's ugliest building for its Brutalist, bare concrete appearance," acknowledges the college website.[176] The thought that came to mind when I first stepped foot inside was that I should be wearing my hard hat, because I was obviously entering a construction zone. More than 50 years later, it's still a building that will never be finished—cold, austere, soulless, but functional.

In addition to constructing authentic-style civic buildings, you need to figure out the general location of city hall, public schools, fire stations, and police stations. This is why you need to choose an outer boundary for your city. Without a fixed boundary, you can't properly site public buildings. It would be like playing a sport on an undefined playing field.

BRAINSTORMING

Determine an outer boundary for your city—what Oregon calls an Urban Growth Boundary and California calls a Sphere of Influence. Then make your chosen land area look like the North American nation it lies within.

This doesn't mean urbanization ends at the line in the sand, it means your city draws a line limiting its jurisdiction to what land it can manage efficiently. Your city should let some other city pick up from where its boundary ends. Los Angeles County has 88 cities within its borders.[177]They each have their own peculiar identity—it's what makes life in the Los Angeles Basin interesting.

If a stranger were to be dropped blindfolded into your city, they should be able to identify which of the Nine Nations of North America they are in. But that is becoming rare as chain retail, chain restaurants, chain housing, and chain society, overpower our regionally distinct cultures. American cities have become "one size fits all" caricatures of the tailor-made cities of the past. Your city should reflect your local history and your local customs—even your local quirks.

5. CHANGING CONDITIONS—LIMITED PLANS

Many of the ways of doing things in the past will not be acceptable in the future. Take waste plastic, for example. Eastman Chemical Company's carbon renewal technology breaks down waste plastics into molecular components such as carbon, oxygen, and hydrogen. Eastman expected to use up to fifty million pounds of waste plastic in carbon renewal technology operations in 2020, and projects are currently underway to significantly expand that amount.[178]

The carbon renewal process breaks down waste plastic to the molecular level and then uses molecular-level "feedstock" to produce new products for markets in textiles, cosmetics, personal care, and ophthalmics (eye drops). With carbon renewal technology, waste plastics can be recycled an infinite number of times without quality degradation. This is a breakthrough we've been hoping for.

BRAINSTORMING

Changing conditions—where do Americans want to live. Many years ago, I attended a planning workshop where slides were projected on a screen by two projectors. Projector "A" would show an urban scene, and then projector "B" would show another urban scene. The audience was instructed to mark on a form which scene they liked best. At the end of the showing, the forms were collected and tabulated. Although the projections showed a wide range of urban scenes, from Manhattan to the Florida Keys, by a wide margin the audience favored scenes of a New England village.

At the end of the workshop, I spoke with the planner who had made the presentation. He told me that every audience in every part of America favored the New England village. For some reason, that's the way our American brains are wired.

In 2018, according to Gallup, Americans given six choices of places to live chose as follows:

27 percent—Rural area

21 percent—Suburb of a big city

17 percent—Small city

12 percent—Big city

12 percent—Town

10 percent—Suburb of a small city[179]

Those are the places where Americans really want to live, but when I look up "the city of the future,"[180] I get pictures of places such as these, all from foreign countries:

- Burj Khalifa, Dubai—2,716 feet high, 163 floors
- Shanghai Tower, Shanghai—2,073 feet high, 126 floors
- Makkah Royal Clock Tower, Mecca—1,972 feet high, 120 floors

None of these megatowers looks like it belongs in the countryside or a New England village.

But once again, architects and the ultra-rich who employ them seem to be at odds with us common folks, who deeply feel the need for peace and quiet and tranquility. We want a snug place to live, not a future living out a nightmare—as in such films as *Escape from New York*, *Escape from Los Angeles*, and *Blade Runner*. Years ago, PBS ran a series about life in the future. The end scene showed a traditional New England village where all the charm was retained and all the technology was hidden from view, undergrounded, or disguised— like those pine tree cell phone towers, only much better. (Personally, I hide my sprinkler controller under a hollow plastic rock.) I hope the New England village turns out to be the real future.

The United States covers about 2.3 billion acres. In 2012, the

United States Department of Agriculture estimated urbanization covered 70 million acres or 3 percent of the land."[181] Plenty of land is available for creating beautiful small towns—we don't need to live all bunched up like bees in a hive—or Borgs in the Hive.

Changing conditions—Workaholics. The international Organization for Economic Co-operation and Development (OECD) defines leisure as a "wide range of indoor and outdoor activities such as walking and hiking, sports, entertainment and cultural activities, socializing with friends and family, volunteering, taking a nap, playing games, watching television, using computers, recreational gardening, etc. Personal care activities include sleeping (but not taking a nap), eating and drinking, and other household or medical or personal services (hygiene, visits to the doctor, hairdresser, etc.) consumed by the respondent. Travel time related to personal care is also included."[182]

HOURS SPENT ON LEISURE AND PERSONAL CARE PER DAY[183]		
Rank	**Country**	**Hours**
1	France	16.36
2	Spain	15.93
3	Netherlands	15.90
4	Denmark	15.87
5	Belgium	15.77

You may have noticed that the United States did not make it into the top 5. We're definitely not number one in leisure—we're way down in thirtieth place. Americans are having a hard time cutting back on the number of hours a week they need to work. In Japan there is a word for "overwork death"—*Karōshi*. You don't need to be the one with the tombstone that says, "I Wish I Had Spent More Time At the Office." Let the robots do the work.

6. BASIC HUMAN NEEDS—LIMITED PLANS

"What is the purpose of life? . . . I believe that the purpose of life is to be happy." —the Dali Lama[184]

What are basic human needs at the local level? Several websites list basic human needs, some list physical needs (Forbes), and others list psychological needs (Uplift). The following list is from author, life coach, and businessman Tony Robbins:

Certainty—assurance that you can avoid pain and gain pleasure

Uncertainty/Variety—the need for the unknown, change, new stimuli

Significance—feeling unique, important, special or needed

Connection/Love—a strong feeling of closeness with someone or something

Growth—an expansion of capacity, capability or understanding

Contribution—a sense of service and focus on helping, giving to and supporting others[226]

Any city should work to meet these basic human needs. After all, the measure of success is happiness, an emotion we all enjoy. If the people of your city are unhappy, you should be sensitive enough to recognize the symptoms and do something about it.

Social justice. Generally speaking, social justice means the fair and equitable distribution of wealth, opportunity, and social privileges between people and their society. Social justice also means the equitable apportionment of taxation, Social Security, public health, public school, public services, labor law, and regulation of markets.

Years ago, I moved to a city in California to serve as an AmeriCorps VISTA volunteer, working with Alzheimer patients. My position was on a college campus on the south side of the city, a less desirable neighborhood. A good friend lived on the north side, a highly desirable area. One day she asked me to drive her to her local library. When we got there, I saw a lavishly landscaped, well-designed concrete building with plenty of books, meeting rooms, and places to enjoy reading. My south side library was a prefabricated plywood box with a few books and no frills. The two libraries were nowhere near equal.

But that is typical of many cities—the wealthier neighborhoods get better services than the poorer areas. The first step you can take is to see if local public services are provided equally to *all* of your neighborhoods. People know when they are being cheated out of their fair share.

A primordial inheritance? Researcher Sarah Brosnan placed pairs of capuchin monkeys next to each other and trained them to hand pebbles to human handlers in exchange for slices of cucumber. After a few exchanges, the first monkey started getting grapes—a tastier treat—while the second monkey continued to get cucumber. Almost immediately the second monkey figured out that it was being cheated and refused to accept any more cucumber. Some monkeys got so mad that they threw uneaten cucumber slices at their handlers.

Repeated studies confirmed that monkeys expect fair treatment—and that that genetic trait is common to other primates as well, including humans. Said Brosnan, "This sense of fairness is the basis of lots of things in human society, from wage discrimination to international politics."[185]

Based on many observations, it looks as though the human response to unfairness may have evolved to support long-term cooperation. It's our cooperative nature that creates the good things in life, not our combativeness. Over time, academics have conducted many laboratory tests on what is called inequity aversion. They consistently find that "people often forgo an available reward because it is not what they expect or think is fair."[186]

A case in point: "Detroiters were refusing city-sponsored 'free trees.' A researcher found out the problem: She was the first person to ask them if they wanted them," reported Brentin Mock for Bloomberg CityLab.[187] One black man described how "green" groups presumed to know what was best for communities of color without including them in the decision-making processes. A quarter of the 7,500 residents who were asked declined to have trees planted in front of their homes. What the researcher found was that the rejections had more to do with how the tree-planters presented themselves and residents' distrust of city government than it did with how they felt about trees.

BRAINSTORMING

Few cities understand the power that resides in communication. For example, my tax bill just says "amount owed: . . ." It *should* list all of the public agencies that benefit from property taxes.

LOCAL GOVERNMENTS RECEIVING REVENUE FROM PROPERTY TAXES		
Cemetery District	Irrigation District	Public Utility District
City Government	K–12 School District	Redevelopment Agency
Community College	Maintenance District	Sanitary District
Community Services	Offices of Education	Street Lighting
County Service Area	Others*	Vector Control District
Fire Protection	Parks and Recreation	Water District
Hospital District	Public Utility District	Wastewater Reclamation

* Thirty-three other special districts share in property tax revenue.

One property tax beneficiary worth mentioning, by the way, is the Vector Control District. These are the folks who come to your home to remove rattlesnakes, coral snakes, scorpions, and the family of skunks that has taken up residency in your garage. They also spray the mosquito larvae in your neighbor's abandoned fishpond. Just about everyone is willing to pay for vector control, once they know what services they provide.

If your city carefully explains what services people are getting for their money, the number of complaints should go way down. Folks like to know what they are paying for.

7. QUALITY OF LIFE—LIMITED PLANS

Quality of life is the expectation of a person to live a good life. The *Encyclopedia Britannica* tells us that "[w]ithin the arena of health care, quality of life is viewed as multidimensional, encompassing emotional, physical, material, and social well-being."

Quality of life at the local level. "The United Nations' Universal Declaration of Human Rights, adopted in 1948, provides an excellent list of factors that can be considered in evaluating quality of life," says Amy Fontinelle on the Investopedia website. "It includes many things that citizens of the United States and other developed countries take for granted, which are not available in a significant number of other countries around the world."[188]

QUALITY OF LIFE INDICATORS	
Freedom from slavery and torture	Freedom of thought
Equal protection under the law	Freedom of religion
Freedom from discrimination	Free choice of employment
Freedom of movement	Right to fair pay
Freedom to reside in one's home country	Equal pay for equal work
Presumption of innocence until proved guilty	Right to vote
Right to marry	Right to rest and leisure
Right to have a family	Right to education
Right to be treated equally	Right to human dignity
Right to privacy	

Even a free country must work at keeping its freedom.

BRAINSTORMING

Open government is your protection against losing your high quality of life.

By law, all city planning permit information is supposed to be freely available to proponents, opponents, advisors, media, and decision-makers—but often that is not how the system actually works. On nearly every occasion when I have contacted city hall asking for the administrative record for a planning permit application, one of those rigid, inflexible, and maladaptive employees will tell me that I am not allowed to see the public documents because they contain "confidential and proprietary" information. I have no idea where city employees pick up this sort of misinformation—of course I, or anyone else, has the right to obtain public documents. I suggest that your city take the following actions to open government to all of us and to protect us from the rigid, inflexible, and maladaptive.

Set up an interactive blog. Around sixty percent of businesses today have blogs. So why shouldn't city hall set up an interactive blog where people can interact, and where public documents such as planning permit applications can be posted?

Lengthen citizen review time. City hall's interactive blog should have a place for planning permit applications to be posted and remain available from the date the planning permit application fees are paid until the last day anyone can legally file an appeal.

Number of days posted on paper at city hall	Processing activity	Number of days if posted on a city blog
	Date application fees are paid	1
	30-day staff review of application	30
10	**Public notice posted for 10 days**	10
	Planning commission hearing date	1
	Appeal period	10
10	Total days	52

PUBLIC ACCESS TO ADMINISTRATIVE RECORDS

Assuming that snail mail delivers the public notice to neighboring property owners in two days, and that rigid, inflexible, and maladaptive clerk hassles you at city hall for two more days, you'll have full access to the administrative record for only six days. But if the administrative record is posted on city hall's blog as it is created, the public, not just neighboring property owners, will have full access to it for a minimum of 52 days. That gives people 30 additional days to complete their fact-finding research before the public hearing date.

In today's information age, information is neither a right nor a privilege; it's a necessity.

Training local leaders. Many local governments are led by people who don't actually know how government works; they just vote their conscience.

Beaver Valley, in Concord Township on the Pennsylvania-Delaware border, has long been valued for its rare beauty, historic significance, and incredible recreational value for hikers, equestrians, and runners. Most people living in the area have always assumed that "the Valley" was owned by a conservation organization called Woodlawn Trustees. However, unknown to all but a few, the property owner was actually Woodlawn, Inc.— a real estate developer, not a caretaker of open space. I found out about this just after the township approved an application to subdivide the land for construction of 171 houses on 230 acres of the Valley. At the public hearing, one township supervisor said, "Every year we select our township professionals, and I have every confidence in the township team. That's why I'm voting yes." Then another township supervisor said she had to rely on the township's consultants for their interpretation of the code.

If the township supervisors had been properly trained in the workings of government, they would have known they were being played for suckers by their trusted consultants and professionals. The application was incomplete and defective; and the subdivision violated many rules and regulations.

In 2016, prosecutors in Beaumont, California, filed embezzlement charges against the former city manager, police chief, public works director, city attorney, economic development and finance director, and city planner for siphoning as much as $43 million from city funds over a period of three decades. District Attorney Mike Hestrin said that the arrests served as a warning against heavily outsourcing city work to private companies. "Cities have to be very careful, and proceed at their own peril, when they invite private companies to be in charge of finance or in charge of their city."[189]

Cities should help their local government leaders get the training they need. Someone has to do it, right? As you have now seen, local leaders don't necessarily know how to protect themselves from unscrupulous advisors and the sharp practices often used by planning permit applicants. Two national organizations offer leadership training, and so do some states. The following are three of the many that are available to local governments.

City council training. The National League of Cities University program builds on core skills for local elected officials and appointed officials through professional training.[190]

Planning commissioner training. The American Planning Association (APA) offers Planning Commissioner Training Guides that help local governments create effective local training programs for planning commissioners. It also offers self-paced, online training for individual planning commissioners.[191]

State-mandated training. Maryland, New York, and some other states require planning commission and board of appeals members to complete courses on their duties and responsibilities.

8. HAPPINESS—LIMITED PLANS

The personal-finance website WalletHub compared more than 180 of the largest U.S. cities for happiness levels in 2019.[192] Topping the list was Plano, Texas, with the lowest unemployment rate (3 percent), one of the lowest poverty rates (7 percent), and a low separation and divorce rate. WalletHub found the unhappiest city to be Detroit, Michigan, with the third-highest unemployment rate (8 percent), highest poverty rate (38 percent), and highest separation and divorce rate (47 percent). In both cities, employment stands out as a key statistic, with poverty being a result. The divorce rate also serves as a measurement of happiness.

As I pointed out back at the beginning of this book, the goal of every business is to generate as much profit as possible and the goal of every city is to supply the necessities of life—food, shelter, medical attention, and protection from harm. Detroit serves as an example of a city that hasn't provided residents with these necessities of life.

Plano—a diversified economy. Plano, Texas, just 20 miles from Dallas, was incorporated in 1873 but didn't grow much until 1970, when it got caught up in the economic boom its neighboring cities were experiencing. During the 1980s, a number of corporations moved their headquarters here, including J. C. Penney and Frito-Lay.[193] Thus far Plano has been able to keep expanding its economy so as to supply those "necessities of life"—food, shelter, medical attention, and protection from harm.

Detroit—single-industry economy. Detroit attracted the automobile industry from the beginning of mass manufacturing, and that came to dominate the city's economy. But the auto industry moved outward from Detroit proper in the 1950s. Detroit was shortsighted in not making a greater attempt to diversify its economy.[194] The city failed to supply those life necessities of food, shelter, medical attention, and protection from harm.

BRAINSTORMING

Your city needs to diversify as much as it possibly can—find ways to attract new employers and workers. This is where branding and creating a sense of place come into play.

Seemingly out of nowhere, the city of Santa Clara, California, became known around the country for its swim club and world-class swimming facility. Founded in 1951 by team coach George Haines, the Santa Clara Swim Club has had such well-known members as Donna de Varona, Pablo Morales, Don Schollander, Mark Spitz, Chris von Saltza, Lynn Burke, George Harrison, Steve Clark, and Paul Hait. Club swimmers have earned 71 Olympic medals—42 gold, 18 silver, and 11 bronze. In 1966 the City of Santa Clara International Swim Center was built, with its training pool, racing pool, and diving well.[195]

There was no reason why the city should have built such a remarkable facility, but it did, and the payoff has been tremendous. Santa Clara has created a brand that attracts young swimmers and their families from around the world. It's creative ideas like this that make one community stand out from the others. What would make *your* city stand out from the herd?

9. SEVEN-GENERATION SUSTAINABILITY—LIMITED PLANS

Seven generations are equal to about 150 years. In the scheme of things, that is not a long time. For example, much of our urban infrastructure lasts for at least 75 years. Some, man-made structures like Roman roads or the Great Wall of China go on for more than a millennium.

My entire neighborhood is 50 years old and most of the original public utilities are in good working order. Your city should always look ahead and consider how long man-made infrastructure and all of the other urban structures will last. Your city should also consider what effect current social services, education and medical care will have on future generations. For example, schooling carries over for multiple generations, leaving behind a trail of educated or uneducated people.

Your city also has to figure out what it will do with the sanitary land fill that is leaking into the groundwater, the Superfund Site and the nuclear power plant that will eventually be decommissioned. Most cities try to kick these problems down the road, but they won't go away.

Chapter 4
THE SPECIFIC PLAN

The third-level city plan is the specific plan, giving directions for land-use development for a selected area and covering every aspect from building design to infrastructure capacity. This is a detailed plan or blueprint for a particular section of the city, and it should answer four questions:

- Where are we now?
- Where do we want to be?
- How do we get there?
- How do we measure our progress?

The specific plan works best if it follows the straightforward principles embodied in the "SMART" formula. SMART is an acronym for the five steps that lead to a goal:

Specific. The goal must be well-defined and focused.

Measurable. The goal must be measurable, using mileposts that quantify progress.

Assignable. The work program must show who will complete the tasks.

Realistic. The work program must show how resources will be allocated to reach the goal.

Time-based. The work program must show in chronological order the events needed to reach the goal.

Using the SMART formula forces a city to incorporate accountability into its third-level plan. Because it leads to physical land development, the specific plan must contend with the legal concept of operational risk—that is, the risk of failure caused by human error, fraud, breach of security or privacy, engineering failure, or ecological mishap. Higher-level plans (the first-level general and second-level limited plans) are low-risk paper plans, but the third-level specific plan involves physical action. It must be carefully thought out ahead of time, with all risks taken into consideration.

The specific plan addresses the same eight parts that the general plan does, as detailed in Chapter 2, but at a more detailed level—the neighborhood level.

SPECIFIC PLANNING AREA

A specific plan should cover a limited area—a square mile (640 acres) or less. Some say it should be based on walking distance. Jarrett Walker, writing in Human Transit says, "If you have to choose a single walking-distance standard for all situations, the most commonly cited standard is 400m or 1/4 mi."[196]

Measuring the land. Before the United States gained its freedom from Great Britain, the colonies recorded property deeds using the British system of cadastral mapping. British cadastral maps described boundaries in "metes and bounds." A map description might read:

"From the point on the north bank of Muddy Creek one mile above the junction of Muddy and Indian Creeks, north for 400 yards, then northwest to the large standing rock, west to the large oak tree, south to Muddy Creek, then down the center of the creek to the starting point."[197]

A metes-and-bounds description had three inherent shortcomings:

- Descriptions were long and convoluted, and they lost currency as generations passed away.
- Boundaries had to be constantly monitored by knowledgeable people with sterling memories; otherwise, boundary rocks might mysteriously move about at night.
- Over time, streams meandered, trees died, and the terrain changed.

When western lands were added to the nation, boundaries were drawn on maps but not marked on the land by monuments such as rocks or trees. To sell uninhabited property, sight unseen, America needed a way to measure land based on fixed coordinates of longitude and latitude rather than local landmarks.

Public Land Survey System. The Public Land Survey System, created in 1785, divides land into squares. First an east-west Geographer's Line is drawn. Then meridians are drawn every 6 miles at right angles to this line, numbered from east to west. Lateral lines are drawn to intersect these meridians at 6-mile intervals. Each square creates a 36-square-mile township, further divided into 36 sections of a square mile each (640 acres). The township became the basic unit of land survey west of New England.

The Public Land Survey System is simple in concept: distance and angles are easy to measure, and it works well when measuring wild or undeveloped land. This system made it possible for the government to record homesteads on vast tracts of empty land sight unseen. (It also made it easy for land speculators and railroads to sell land they had never seen to immigrants fresh off the boat.) Out of convenience, country roads were spaced a half-mile apart. Fortuitously, dividing the land into squares and spacing roads this way creates a convenient street system for an urban area. Over time, country roads evolved into a gridwork of streets, with arterial streets spaced half a mile apart. That turned out to work very well when public transportation came along.[198]

PUBLIC LAND SURVEY SYSTEM			
	Miles	**Square Miles**	**Acres**
Quadrangle	24 by 24	576	368,640
Township	6 by 6	36	23,040
Section	1 by 1	1	640
Half-section	1 by 1/2	1/2	320
Quarter-section	1/2 by 1/2	1/4	160
Half of quarter-section	1/2 by 1/4	1/8	80
Quarter of quarter-section	1/4 by 1/4	1/16	40

Because so much of America has been laid out using the Public Land Survey System, most specific plans can be expected to be bounded by squares.

Population per square mile. Population density varies widely from city to city in the U.S., and even across different neighborhoods within a single city. New York City's density is almost 28,000 people per square mile, while that of Los Angeles is about 8,300 people per square mile. The chart below shows the population per square mile for a few American cities:[199]

POPULATION PER SQUARE MILE, 2017	
New York City	28,000
San Francisco	18,000
Los Angeles	8,300
Phoenix	3,000
Memphis	2,000

When thinking about the boundaries for a specific plan, a square mile with a population of around 4,000 people may be a realistic size. A planning area larger than that is likely too large for most people to envision.

SPECIFIC PLAN CONTENT

A specific plan, as defined by the State of California, includes detailed text and diagrams that explain the scope of the plan, including the following:

Land use. The distribution, location, and extent of land uses—measuring the land area.

Transportation. The distribution, location, and extent of air, ground and water transportation.

Public utilities. The distribution, location, and extent of water, sewage, drainage, solid waste, gas, and electric, utilities.

Standards and criteria. Rules and regulations that control construction, demolition and conservation of structures; and rules and regulations that control conservation, development, and utilization of natural resources.

Funding process. Funding measures to implement the plan.

California also added some additional questions to help define the content of the specific plan—though some of these may be addressing the past rather than the future, as I've questioned in my parenthetical comments:

1. Is the planning area a complete and integrated community containing housing, shops, workplaces, schools, parks, and civic facilities essential to residents' daily life?
2. Is the planning area designed so that housing, jobs, daily needs, and other activities are within easy walking distance of each other?
3. Is the area within easy walking distance of transit stops? And

is it part of a larger transit network? (*But does your city actually have a dense enough population to justify mass transit? Mass transit requires very high-density urban development. And I've made it clear that I favor autonomous vehicles.*)

4. Will the area provide a diversity of housing for a wide range of economic levels and age groups?

5. Will the area provide a range of jobs?

6. Will the area have a central focus area combining commercial, civic, cultural, and recreational uses?

7. Will the area provide "islands" in the form of squares, greens, and parks to foster a sense of place—focal points that break up monotony—in comparison to the uniformity of suburbia?

8. Will there be public spaces that attract people's attention and presence at all hours of the day and night? (*Mainstream planning assumes that all of us will soon be living in cities as densely populated as Manhattan. However, evidence points toward continued American-style low-density urbanization.*)

9. Will the area have a well-defined edge, such as an agricultural greenbelt or a wildlife corridor, that is permanently protected from development?

10. Will the area have low-speed local streets, pedestrian paths, and bike paths that follow interesting routes to popular destinations?

11. Will the area be designed to encourages safe pedestrian and bicycle use by being human-scaled and spatially defined by buildings, trees, and lighting?

12. Will high-speed traffic be eliminated from local streets by including speed control in the area's street design? (*Autonomous vehicles automatically obey speed limits!*)

13. Is the area going to reclaim or preserve the natural terrain, drainage, and vegetation by creating parks or greenbelts as part of the public infrastructure?

14. Will resources be conserved and waste minimized?

15. Will efficient use of water be provided through natural drainage, drought-tolerant landscaping, and recycling?
16. Will streets and buildings be oriented to maximize natural summer shading, thus reducing mechanical air-conditioning and saving electricity?

FORM-BASED CODE CONTENT

The term "Form-Based Coding" was introduced at a 2001 Chicago zoning commission presentation by Carol Wyant, who served as executive director of the Form-Based Code Institute when it was established in 2004 by private-practice planners competing with public-agency planners for work.

According to the Form-Based Codes Institute: "A form-based code is a land development regulation that fosters predictable built results and a high-quality public realm by using physical form (rather than separation of uses) as the organizing principle for the code."[200] The concept is presented in the book *Form Based Codes: A Guide for Planners, Urban Designers, Municipalities, and Developers* by Daniel Parolek, Karen Parolek, and Paul Crawford.[201]

- A form-based code generally addresses these issues:
- A glossary of the precise use of terms
- A project application and review process
- A plan showing where different building form standards apply
- Specifications for sidewalks, street lighting, street parking, travel lanes, street trees, street furniture, and so on
- Regulations that control the configuration, features, and functions of buildings

The following supplementary issues may also be addressed by a form-based code:

- Regulations for external architectural materials and quality

- Regulations for landscape design and plant materials, parking lot screening, street corner sight lines, pedestrian movements, etc.
- Regulations for sign dimensions, materials, illumination, and placement
- Regulations for storm water drainage and infiltration, hillside development, tree protection, solar access, etc.[202]

The Form-Based Code institute now speaks for many architects, urban designers, and planners who sell their services to local governments. Backers of the code claim that it replaces Euclidian zoning, but in practice form-based codes are very much like specific plans and can be used as an alternative. In fact, form-based code plans are sometimes much more creative.

Chapter 5

THE EMERGENCY PLAN

The emergency plan plots out the course of action that needs to be followed if the city's plan fails or the assumed future changes. Not many governments develop effective emergency plans. After all, what could possibly go wrong? Flood, fire, earthquake, drought . . .

A well-thought-out emergency plan can have far-reaching consequences. It allows city work crews to practice how they will respond when disaster strikes, and it prompts the city to budget for supplies and equipment to use in emergencies. "You haven't seen any face masks around here, have you?"

On December 23, 1972, an earthquake with a magnitude of 6.2 struck Managua, Nicaragua, killing 5,000 people, injuring 20,000, and leaving 250,000 homeless. American Peace Corps nurses in Central America were immediately sent to Managua. When they arrived, they found the hospital destroyed. Soon U.S. Military canvas-tent field hospitals arrived, but when they were unpacked, the nurses found that the autoclaves used to sterilize surgical instruments were missing. Someone had forgotten to pack them.

The Managua earthquake serves as an example of why emergency plans are essential. Where were the autoclaves? How could replacements be sent to Managua? Meanwhile, the nurses were cleaning with soap and water and alcohol.

The emergency plan is a proactive approach as opposed to crisis management, which is the reactive approach. A proactive emergency plan ensures that you're always prepared ahead of time, whereas reactive crisis management is literally plugging the hole in the dike *after* the flood.

FOR RISKS YOU CAN IDENTIFY

An emergency plan can only address risks that you are able to identify. That's why so many cities don't have emergency plans—they tell themselves that they can't foretell the future. But you need to try.

The Houston Chronicle reported in September 2019, "As the flood-weary city of Houston recovers from yet another historic storm in the coming days, rubber-gloved mucking brigades and tow truck armies will swoop in to clean up the physical mess. But more and more, Houstonians are finding that the toll of these repeated floods reaches far beyond the physical. The events have changed the very way our city feels. . . . Harvey was the third '500-year' rain event to hit Southeast Texas in three years. . . . And many residents are now asking themselves: Is Houston worth it?"[203]

In California, according to *Mother Jones* magazine in 2019, "For countless generations, Indigenous people have worked with fire to maintain healthy landscapes that are less prone to massive wildfires. While allowing natural fires to burn, Native Americans in California and elsewhere started some intentionally to clear dry brush, maintain species balance, and create prairies and meadows where animals graze."[204] But now, according to a 2019 article in Forbes, "This is California's big secret: it's not climate change that's burning up the forests . . . it's decades of environmental mismanagement that has created a tinderbox of unharvested timber, dead trees, and thick underbrush."[205]

THE FEDERAL READY CAMPAIGN

"Ready" is a national public service campaign developed to help communities respond to natural and man-made disasters. The goal is to advance preparedness through public involvement. Ready can provide you with all the information you need to develop an emergency plan (https://www.ready.gov/business/implementation/emergency).

Emergency plans fit nicely into the seven-generation concept (discussed in chapter 1): "Look and listen for the welfare of the whole people and have always in view not only the present but also the coming generations, even those whose faces are yet beneath the surface of the ground—the unborn of the future Nation."

Chapter 6
APPLIED PLANNING

From this point forward I will be discussing how local plans advance from being abstract ideas written on paper to becoming physical objects manifest on the land. Either a specific plan or a form-based code (as discussed in Chapter 4) may be employed to advance a written proposal to its physical manifestation. Both achieve the same results.

The following two chapters go into detail about redevelopment plans and preservation plans, both of which are neighborhood-based. So, the first step in planning is to determine exactly what constitutes a neighborhood.

DEFINE YOUR NEIGHBORHOOD

There is no English word that adequately describes the land area called a neighborhood. When someone talks about their neighborhood, they may be talking about their social neighborhood or about the administrative district the government calls a neighborhood. Often the government's administrative district is larger than their social neighborhood, though in some places they may have the same boundaries. It can be confusing.

In the United States, people often live-in neighborhoods of between 6,000 to 30,000 people, and they seem to feel comfortable with that.

San Francisco—America's second most densely populated city—recognizes 27 administrative neighborhoods, with an average population of about 30,000 people. The average size of a designated neighborhood in San Francisco is 1.75 square miles.[206] Los Angeles, a city known for urban sprawl, recognizes about 208 administrative neighborhoods with an average population density of about 19,000 people.[207] The average size of a neighborhood in Los Angeles is 2.4 square miles. Of course, this being la-la land, every website I visited listed a different number of neighborhoods.

Looking at urban places worldwide suggests that people can feel a sense of community living in neighborhoods of around 6,000 to 30,000 people, covering 2 or 3 square miles.

In France, there are 95 suburbs or neighborhoods (*cités* or *banlieues*) surrounding Paris and located within the first four zones of the city's public transportation system. Combined, the suburbs have a population of around 775,000, or an average of about 8,000 people per administrative neighborhood.

And in China, state officials throughout different dynasties chose to control life and activity at the neighborhood level. Even today, under the current communist rule, people are sorted into localities of 2,000 to 10,000 families, so administrative neighborhood population works out to be around 6,000 to 30,000 people. (The number of family members in a home has declined from 5.3 in the 1950s to 3.02 in 2012.)[208]

A SENSE OF COMMUNITY

According to the theory put forth by psychologists David McMillan and David Chavis, four elements need to be present if a person is to feel a sense of community:

Membership. The individual feels a sense of belonging and identification, personal investment, boundaries, emotional safety, and shares a common symbol system.

Influence. Group cohesion arises from a feeling that the individual can influence the group, and likewise that the group can influence the individual.

Integration and need fulfillment. The individual feels rewarded for participating with the group.

Shared emotional connection. The individual feels a bond of shared history with the group.[209]

In any reasonably sized neighborhood, all but the most isolated people seem to be able to pick up on what's going on by reading the local newspaper, listening to talk radio, blogging, surfing the net, gossiping with neighbors, being hounded by busybodies trying to get them to sign petitions, reading leaflets stuck to car windshields, and many other wanted or unwanted interactions.

Back in the 1950s, after my family moved out of San Francisco, we lived in a nearby 5-square-mile suburb of 20,000 people. Every kid knew that the town was informally divided into two neighborhoods, and we all knew that White Oak Way was the street that separated the two. We always felt we were going out of our neighborhood when we crossed that street. Every kid also knew how far was too far to walk or ride their bike. Studies show that a typical walking rate for school-age children is about 1.35 miles in 30 minutes, so a neighborhood of around 2.5 square miles is about the right size for walking children. Studies also show that a typical child bikes at 8 miles per hour, taking them about 4 miles in 30 minutes—but most kids on bikes don't venture beyond the distance they can walk, they just get to their destination faster.[210]

EVERY NEIGHBORHOOD NEEDS A NAME

Telling someone that you live in Los Angeles means nothing at all—it's like saying you live on Earth. The *Los Angeles Times* lists 272 neighborhoods within the city.[211] (The city itself recognizes about 208 administrative neighborhoods.) You have to say which of the 272 you live in if you want someone to know where you "really" live.

A few years ago, when we lived in Palm Springs, the city started putting up street signs identifying its neighborhoods. (We lived in the Gene Autry Neighborhood.) The city also formed neighborhood associations with elected officers whom we could count on to get the word out to us.

It's a good idea to name your city's neighborhoods based on a theme. You can name them after trees, animals, or birds—but not politicians or Confederate war leaders.

CITY PLANNING IMPLEMENTATION

There are only three ways to move city planning from concept to action:

- Planning permission—means obtaining a permit granted by the city to carry out development.
- Redevelopment—means replacing blight with beneficial land uses funded by selling tax allocation bonds.
- Preservation—means replacing blight with beneficial land uses funded by selling general obligation bonds or funding with money on hand.

The vast majority of city building occurs through day-to-day planning permit processing which includes issuing building permits, subdivision permits, planned unit development permits or adopting local plan amendments. The planning department routinely processes these permits.

Redevelopment and preservation are undertaken by your city exercising its police power granted by the Tenth Amendment to the U. S. Constitution, which gives local governments the power to establish and enforce laws protecting the welfare, safety, and health of the public.

FINANCING NEIGHBORHOOD PLANS

The two next chapters talk about neighborhood redevelopment and preservation plans. A redevelopment plan is often based on a neighborhood of around 6,000 to 30,000 people, covering 2 or 3 square miles, but individual project areas are generally limited to about 200 acres, or about three project areas per square mile. I've worked as a planner on five redevelopment projects: Bayview Redevelopment (242 acres), El Portal Redevelopment (248 acres), Sheffield Redevelopment (32 acres), Central Redevelopment (185 acres), and Hillside Redevelopment (370 acres). Each of these projects was completed in fewer than five years, and all were very profitable to the city and made the community a much better place to live.

A preservation plan may also be based on neighborhoods of about 6,000 to 30,000 people, covering 2 or 3 square miles. But because a preservation plan doesn't use tax allocation bonds (a.k.a. tax increment financing), with all of the tax sharing and rigmarole that entails, some project areas cover a full 2 or 3 square miles. But I recommend sticking with smaller land areas of about 200 acres.

Redevelopment plan. To fund a redevelopment plan, the local city or county government sells tax allocation bonds to investors. The following is my interpretation of the state of Washington's bureaucratic gobbledygook:[212]

- A city may issue tax allocation bonds for the financing of public improvements.
- The principal and interest of tax allocation bonds is payable from tax allocation revenues and project revenues such as income, fees, and rents from the public improvement financed with the proceeds of the bonds.
- Tax allocation bonds are not the general obligation of or guaranteed by the full faith and credit of the city, and are not considered to be the city's debt.

And that is about as simple as I can make it. In practice, a city (or county) passes an ordinance creating a redevelopment agency corporation. This corporation operates as a legally separate entity from the city, even though the corporate board of directors usually consists of the same people who serve on the city council (though they may be completely different people—family, friends, etc.).

By separating the city from the redevelopment agency, blame can be spread around when things go wrong. In any event, the thing to remember is that when things go wrong and there's not enough money in the pot to pay back the bondholders, the city can just walk away.

Preservation plan. A city funds a preservation plan by selling general obligation bonds to investors, payment of which is guaranteed by the full faith and credit of the city. General obligation bonds obligate the people who live in the city to take financial responsibility for paying off the debt—which is why it can be so difficult to pass a bond issue at election time.

Whistle-stop financing. In 1880 a whistle-stop was created in Arizona when the railroad came through. The place had never amounted to much in the past, and it still defies growth and prosperity. But a few years ago, a real estate speculator came up with a scheme to build a 20,000-resident retirement destination on the edge of town—out in the surrounding desert. He needed cash to get his dream built, So he went to city hall and sweet-talked the locals into financing his dream.

Unlike other states, Arizona doesn't allow cities to sell tax allocation bonds, but that didn't kill the proposal. The local folks saw the gold they'd been seeking for nearly 150 years—jobs for the 25 percent of the folks in town who always seem to be without work. So, they agreed to finance the entire retirement development by issuing general obligation bonds that local property owners will have to repay over time. This has the effect of making everyone in town responsible for the debt, while the real estate speculator will be responsible for raking in the profit.

The arrangement is probably not going to end well—but what the heck.

Not easy money. General obligation bonds, bake sales, and raffles are not easy ways to raise cash for local planning, so a preservation plan has to advance slowly and deliberately rather than boldly, the way a redevelopment plan can. Consequently, neighborhood preservation planning ends up looking like the mirror image of redevelopment—you have to do the cheap and easy stuff first and the hard stuff last.

BASIC FIELD WORK—SORTING

"The Sorting Hat is one of the cleverest enchanted objects most witches and wizards will ever meet."

—J.K. Rowling (Harry Potter)

Once your city defines and names its neighborhoods, it is time to decide which individual properties add value to your city and which individual properties are out of place and need to be rehabilitated or demolished.

Sorting is done by walking the neighborhood, with or without your sorting hat, photographing properties and checking one of three boxes:

- **Good.** Properties that present the neighborhood look and feel the city wants to preserve and protect. For example, the look and feel of American Craftsman style architecture, a.k.a. American Arts and Crafts architecture of the 1890s to about1930.

- **Fair.** Properties that need to be repaired, remodeled or restored so that they look like the American Craftsman style architecture the city wants to preserve and protect. These are properties that show signs of neglect such as deteriorated roofing, peeling paint, makeshift additions, inappropriate façade treatments, aluminum siding, ill-fitting replacement windows, and garish painting and decorating. I've found that many run-down properties are rentals being milked for short term profits.

- **Poor.** Properties that need to be demolished and replaced with new construction that looks like the American Craftsman style architecture that the city wants to preserve and protect. Properties in poor condition just don't fit in such as odd shaped structures, home-made additions, mixed architectural styles, storefronts from a different era (or planet), sign structures and lighting fixtures that detract from the historic streetscape, and totemic architecture—Golden Arches, Sonic drive-in, and Jack-in-the-Box.

Remember, the sorting can be done successfully by as few as three people walking the neighborhood, photographing properties and checking boxes. The three sorters combined should be able to reach consensus on which properties fit into which category—what stays and what goes. The giant holding the muffler in his arms is probably not going to make the cut.

After the sorting, a construction estimator should be able to accurately determine project costs using one of the available industry publications.

The whole sorting and cost estimating task takes only a few days to complete. It is not very complicated. I've done this five times, so I know how easy it is to do.

Chapter 7
THE REDEVELOPMENT PLAN

A redevelopment plan differs from a preservation plan in only one way: it is funded by tax allocation bonds (a.k.a. tax increment financing). Without tax allocation bonds, there is just not enough cash available to get rid of blight and rebuild with the highest and best land uses. Every state except for California and Arizona allows tax allocation bonds. So those two states are locked out of the game.

The redevelopment agency sells bonds based on the estimated future value of the real estate after redevelopment is completed. If all goes well, the bondholders earn a profit, if not, they lose their money. The redevelopment agency just fades away into bankruptcy. The city itself is not a party to the transactions and has no obligation to the bond holders.

By definition, "redevelopment" is the elimination and replacement of blight with higher-value land use that will increase the value of real estate located in the project area. On the other hand, many poorly run redevelopment projects have led to a loss of local historical continuity and sense of place. The most striking losses occur when a familiar place such as an historic downtown is demolished and replaced by an incongruous suburban shopping mall.

REDEVELOPMENT AGENCY AND FREE ENTERPRISE

The free enterprise economic system is characterized by the freedom to seek profit in competitive conditions. A well-run redevelopment agency will operate as much like a free enterprise business as the law allows. Redevelopment is neither a social service agency nor a charity. A redevelopment agency is a government agency composed of the following three distinct businesslike components, none of which should ever be thought of as a social service.

Real estate broker. A redevelopment agency is a real estate brokerage business. It may appraise property, market property, manage property, exchange property, auction property, and prepare contracts and leases.

Real estate developer. A redevelopment agency is also a real estate development business. It buys land and readies it for construction. The developer may also employ design professionals and construction contractors, subdivide the property, install infrastructure, and erect structures.

Real estate lender. A redevelopment agency is also a real estate finance business. It may provide short-term acquisition, development, and construction financing (AD&C) and lend money for renovation. It may also acquire federal and state grants and pass subsidies on to end users. The revolving loan fund is replenished when individual projects repay their loans and the money can be reloaned. Theoretically, money should both accumulate and perpetuate in an endless loop, but graft and corruption seem to find ways to prevent that from happening.

VISION, THEME, WORK PLAN, TIMELINE

By definition, redevelopment is used to increase the value of a parcel of real estate by eliminating blight and replacing it with a high-er-value land use. But that doesn't say much. By definition, cooking is the process of preparing food by applying heat, but just as there is much more to cooking than that, so there is much more to redevelopment than knocking down old buildings and putting up new ones. Important elements in both cases are techniques—the procedures used to accomplish an activity—and good judgment. Knowing how to apply technique is the difference between success and failure, soup or goop. Redevelopment requires the proper application of technique based on a vision, a theme, a work plan, and a timeline schedule.

Vision. An important talent of design professionals is the creative ability to visualize a finished project in their mind's eye. Redevelopment agencies need people in positions of responsibility who have this ability. Otherwise, the agency will have no idea where it is going or what it is doing.

Theme. Redevelopment is more than just tearing down old buildings and putting up new ones. Redevelopment must set out an overall design theme and aim to create a unique or recognizable setting, the way Walt Disney set out to create Disneyland. Viable themes can run anywhere from "Main Street U.S.A." to "Tomorrowland."

Work plan. A detailed plan of action cannot be vague or ill defined; it must be a buildable proposal that includes detailed designs, precise costs, and realistic marketing. You must have a written-in-blood, will-to-win battle plan.

Timeline. There must be a timeline showing the sequence of the redevelopment events from inception to completion. Without a firm timeline, redevelopment will linger on without direction. My hands-on experience has taught me that a redevelopment project must be completed within five years.

THE PRIME DIRECTIVE

In Gene Roddenberry's *Star Trek* universe, the "Prime Directive" prohibits Starfleet personnel from interfering with the internal development of alien civilizations.[213] In the redevelopment universe, the prime directive is to eliminate blight first.

Gresham's law is an economic principle often stated as "bad money drives out good."[214] But what was originally an economic principle has been found to apply to redevelopment as well: blight drives away businesses, customers, and residents. Blight acts like the bacteria or fungi that decompose tissue. Urban blight can be briefly defined as the physical deterioration of real property that occurs when the fair market value falls below the equity of the property, or when income from property is lower than expenses. This is often referred to as an upside-down mortgage—the value is less than the amount owed, creating negative equity.

Most states are flexible when it comes to defining blight, often deferring to the judgment of the locality proposing redevelopment. Pennsylvania law states: "Power of discretion over what areas are to be considered blighted is solely within power of the redevelopment authority."[215]

Time is of the essence. The secret of successful redevelopment is to move with all deliberate speed. The quicker city hall acts to eliminate blight, the sooner the blighted area will return to good socioeconomic health. The same speed must be applied to reconstruction and sale to the end users. Time wasted is opportunity missed. If a redevelopment project isn't completed in five years or less, momentum will be lost—and so will city hall's credibility.

REDEVELOPMENT MUST BE PROFITABLE

Profit comes from moving quickly enough to complete the work before the economic cycle becomes unfavorable. New development must produce significantly more revenue than the blight it replaces. A redevelopment agency is in essence a real estate developer and must abide by the rules of the real estate market. Each of the five redevelopment projects I've completed turned a profit. I cringe when I see redevelopment agencies "give away the store" by writing down redevelopment land—it's a formula for failure.

One of the earliest theorists of what would eventually be called political economy, Ibn Khaldun (1332–1406) said that to maximize profits you must buy at a low price and sell at a high price. Sounds simple enough to me, but most redevelopment agencies fail to grasp the concept. They do just the opposite. It's called land write-down, turning Ibn Khaldun's "Buy Cheap, Sell Dear" principle into "Buy Dear, Sell Cheap."

Buy dear, sell cheap—Minnesota. The Minnesota Tax Increment Financing Glossary (tax allocation bonds) says that a Housing and Redevelopment Authority "may acquire a parcel for $1 million and spend an additional $100,000 demolishing a building on the property. If the HRA sells the property to a developer for $500,000, the price of the land is 'written down' from the HRA's $1.1 million cost to $500,000. The authority may give the land to the developer—i.e., "write it down to zero."[216]

Buy dear, sell cheap—California. Following this same logic, CRA/LA (successor to the defunct Community Redevelopment Agency of the City of Los Angeles) says roughly the same thing: "The lowering of land prices by a redevelopment agency occurs when the agency assumes part of the acquisition, demolition, and improvement costs because it imposes more stringent development requirements on the land. The difference between the market value and the fair re-use value for the uses and restrictions proposed by the redevelopment agency is commonly known as land write-down."[217]

PUBLIC NUISANCE LAWS

As defined by *The Free Dictionary*, "The term public nuisance covers a wide variety of minor crimes that threaten the health, morals, safety, comfort, convenience, or welfare of a community. Violators may be punished by a criminal sentence, a fine, or both. A defendant may also be required to remove a nuisance or to pay the costs of removal."[218]

Virtually every local government has the authority to enact a local public nuisance ordinance that requires all property owners within the jurisdiction to maintain their real estate in good repair. If owners allow their property to become blighted, they must restore it to a state of good repair; if they fail to do so, local government has the authority to place a lien on the property to recover the cost of eliminating the blight. Owners may voluntarily sell or donate the blighted real estate to the local government, for the appraised value or less—never more. If owners continue to maintain their property in a blighted condition, local government may exercise its powers of eminent domain. No matter what, the blight must go first.

Problem 1: getting rid of blight. *Question:* Why would a redevelopment agency pay, let's say, $1 million and then spend $100,000 clearing away someone else's blight? *Answer:* If a developer is only willing to pay $500,000 for the land with the blight removed and the site ready for rebuilding, the redevelopment agency paid too much for the land and the blight.

If city hall, acting as the redevelopment agency, finds a property to be a public nuisance (blighted), it has the authority to order the owner to demolish, remove, or clear the nuisance. If the owner fails to do so, the redevelopment agency itself has the authority to act. If a redevelopment agency pays to abate the nuisance, it also has the authority to place a lien on the property until the owner pays for the blight removal. That's the law everywhere in the United States. I don't see anything in the law about the redevelopment agency paying $1 million to a lawbreaker, then spending $100,000 of our tax money to clean up after the lawbreaker's mess.

I've worked on five redevelopment projects from start to finish, and in all five cases the owners of the blighted properties were more than willing to give their property to the redevelopment agency just to get out from under their legal liability.

Problem 2: writing down land. *Question:* Why would a redevelopment agency sell property to a developer for $500,000 or less if it is worth more? *Answer:* Redevelopment agencies sell land for less than it is worth because they want to be loved.

In his book *A Theory of Human Motivation,*[219] Abraham Maslow included in his "hierarchy of needs" the need for "love and belonging." According to Josh Clark in "Why do we love?" (from the website HowStuffWorks), a 2005 study using functional magnetic resonance imaging (fMRI) confirmed Maslow's theory. It found visual evidence that the brain releases dopamine into a region of the reward system called the "nucleus acumens."[220]

Anyone who attends decision-making meetings on a regular basis can tell you that the act of voting "yes" is an act of love. When a decision-maker votes "yes," the brain releases dopamine into a region of the reward system. Watch the dopamine flow as decision-makers raise their hands to grant approval—I swear you can see it in their eyes. The next time you see that gaga look on a decision-maker's face, you will know what it means.

Some very successful property development firms have honed their ability to use our basic need for love and belonging in order to consummate lucrative deals with naive and trusting redevelopment agencies. These upper-echelon confidence men use clever and untrue statements to charm redevelopment agencies into writing down land.

There's no such thing as a free lunch. Redevelopment must not be wasted on unprofitable ventures such as new government buildings and sports stadiums. A few years ago, I talked to a former city council member who bragged to me how, back before the housing bubble and the stock market crash, the local redevelopment agency had paid for a new city hall, library, senior center, youth center, and skateboard park. All well and good—but then he went on to lament how the redevelopment agency had slid into insolvency, having done nothing much to revive the declining economy.

Sadly, many cities across the country divert redevelopment funds that are sorely needed to revive the local economy into money-losing freebies: the devil makes them do it! For many years, the city of San Bernardino, California, balanced its budget by siphoning off $6 million a year from its redevelopment agency. When then-Governor Jerry Brown abolished California's redevelopment agencies in 2011, the gravy train suddenly pulled out of the station, leaving the city with a budget deficit of about $45 million. San Bernardino went bankrupt. According to the 2010 U.S. Census, nearly 46 percent of the city's 200,000 residents received some form of government assistance. Then-Mayor Pat Morris said, "We've been living on the financial edge for a long, long time. But we were unmasked by the meltdown in 2007 when we lost $16 million in sales tax in one year, when we lost 60 percent of our land value and 5,000 homes went into foreclosure."[221]

Three redevelopment vignettes. In the following paragraphs, I present three redevelopment vignettes. Two were inspired by leaders with the vision and the courage to take bold action. Without bold action, guided by smart thinking, neither would have succeeded. The third is an example of a failed redevelopment situation.

Project one. An older residential neighborhood adjacent to a city's central business district had become blighted. The neighborhood suffered from the intermingling of low-value, worn-out commercial and industrial buildings with new residential development. City hall undertook a 242-acre community redevelopment project, replacing older commercial and industrial buildings with new housing and rehabilitating older housing to meet current code requirements. City hall took the initiative to finance all of the risky new construction projects. Redevelopment was completed in less than five years and returned a substantial profit to city hall.

Project two. A small city in the San Francisco Bay Area petitioned the federal government back in the 1970s for urban renewal funds. The government turned the city down, saying it would be throwing good money after bad; at that time the city had a murder rate ten times higher than New York City's. Out of desperation, the city mortgaged city hall (a condemned school building) to raise seed money for a 248-acre community redevelopment project. The locally funded project rehabilitated the central business district along Main Street— previously characterized by low-value "strip commercial" development where each store had its own parking lot and street access. In most cases, as blighted buildings were demolished, new construction started the next day so that lots weren't left vacant. In one instance, a small financial services office was demolished and replaced with a prefabricated building over a four-day weekend—no work time was lost. (Many customers were left questioning their sanity: "I don't remember this office looking like this.") At the completion of redevelopment, the city still had only about 216 local businesses, but retail sales had increased many times over, creating many new jobs. The project returned a substantial profit to city hall.

Project three. On the other hand, there are scores of failed redevelopment projects all across the country. Some of the worst are summarized in a 2006 report from the Castle Coalition (a group that helps organize legal challenges of eminent domain), "Redevelopment Wrecks: 20 Failed Projects Involving Eminent Domain Abuse."[222] When I read about these disasters, I came across one that I know quite well: the Indio Fashion Mall in Southern California.

According to the Castle Coalition, the Indio Fashion Mall had been losing traffic to the trendier Westfield Shoppingtown in nearby Palm Desert since it opened in the mid-70s. The mall lies on 16 acres in front of 17 city-owned acres acquired through eminent domain in 1988. To accommodate mall expansion, the city razed some 80 homes, several stores, and a low-income housing project. When expansion plans collapsed, Indio tried again with a different developer—who asked for even more land. The developer purchased the mall in November 2003, planning to transform it into a destination shopping center. "Immediately, city officials announced their intention to purchase seven lots that the government's wrecking ball spared in 1988, including three churches. According to City Manager Glenn Southard, as of May 2006, all of the land for the redevelopment plan had been acquired or was in escrow. The city obtained the land by threatening eminent domain because [the developer] promised 'sales tax for the city.' The mall project has been a dismal failure, and the city may be setting itself up for more disappointment."[223]

Indio lies halfway between Los Angeles and Yuma, Arizona. It came into existence because the railroad needed a watering station; one was built in California's Coachella Valley in the 1870s and eventually grew into the town of Indio. I first visited in 1963, when it was still a farm community of around 10,000 people and I was a college student working a summer job in the area. I still think of Indio as a small, slow-moving desert community where temperatures reach 125 degrees and people stayed out of the sun during the day and took siestas. Now, with central air conditioning, Indio has become a retirement town and a tourist destination for "snow birds" looking for respite from the cold.

Indio's population has grown to about 85,000, doubling since 1990. Sadly, the town has become unrecognizable to me (though we regularly shopped there when we lived in Palm Springs), mainly because of mindless urban sprawl and lack of planning. Long ago, Indio's most enjoyable feature was the canopy of trees that shaded everyone from the scorching desert heat. But the new suburban tract houses don't need shade, being air-conditioned down to near freezing, and the only landscaping seems to be shadeless palm trees and colored gravel. In the mid-1960s, Indio's civic and political leaders let a series of outside consultants talk them into redevelopment that eliminated the community's charm and functionality by doing the following:

- Failing to protect the citywide canopy of trees that pedestrians relied on for cooling shade, allowing street trees and specimen trees to die out and replacing shade with sunburn.
- Allowing haphazard strip commercial development to line the

state highway, creating traffic hazards and an overabundance of neon signs.

- Bulldozing the entire picturesque central business district and replacing the charming downtown with a nondescript suburban mall.

Forty years later, the mall has failed and weed-choked vacant lots are about all that remains of the old downtown. But that's what can happen when city leaders trust any outside developer who comes along with a promise of sales taxes for the city.

One last comment: What about those 17 acres behind the shopping center that the city acquired in 1988? Back in the 1930s, Dr. Reynaldo Carreon—Indio's first doctor—transferred a large parcel of land to John Nobles, a black man, at a time when selling land to blacks was forbidden by deed restrictions. In time, the John Nobles Ranch became a thriving neighborhood where black families could buy land and build their own homes and businesses. But in 1988, at the request of the Indio Fashion Mall, the redevelopment agency used eminent domain to condemn the neighborhood and relocate residents against their wishes, though they fought back tenaciously with help from the NAACP. By 1993 the last holdouts were forced to resettle elsewhere, ending their longstanding community. It's all gone now, and it turns out the land wasn't even needed for the mall. Last time I looked, it was 17 acres of vacant land, serving no purpose whatsoever except to wreck a viable community and lose a lot of local history.

WHERE CITIZEN PARTICIPATION COMES IN

As an involved citizen, it shouldn't be difficult for you to figure out if a redevelopment proposal has a vision, a theme, a work plan, and a timeline schedule. If any one of these four is missing or ill defined, you need to question city hall and demand a straightforward answer. If city hall can't come up with the facts, don't be part of the flock of sheep: protest the proposal before your community is wrecked.

Back to the prime directive. Never lose sight of the prime directive of redevelopment: to eliminate blight. If a proposal dances around the question of who will eliminate the blight and how it will be done, watch out. Be aware that *blight must be eliminated before new buildings can be constructed.* Just filling in empty lots with new buildings (called "infill development") won't work.

Time is of the essence. Look for a real schedule, not just a vague statement that says state law provides for a 10-year completion timeline, plus extensions. Five years should be the outer limit. Beyond that, enthusiasm will wane and momentum will be lost.

Redevelopment should be profitable. Redevelopment is real estate development that replaces less profitable with more profitable land use, or what the real estate profession calls the "highest and best use." A redevelopment agency is just another real estate developer trying to make a buck. Don't let some do-gooder (the bane of redevelopment agencies) tell you that redevelopment is a charity: it is not!

REDEVELOPMENT AS A ZERO-SUM GAME

According to the American Planning Association's *Policy Guide on Public Redevelopment*, "In some people's minds, the original purposes of redevelopment—the provision of safe, sanitary, and affordable housing, the elimination of blight, and the revitalization of local economies—have been replaced by a zero-sum game. In this game, communities compete for increasingly small shares of retail activity by pouring redevelopment resources into retail recruitment and attraction."[224] The zero-sum game does not benefit the common good.

A zero-sum game is when one player's gain is equal to another player's loss, so that the net change is zero. One example would be when "Boeing, the world's largest maker of commercial aircraft, chose Chicago [for its new headquarters location] over Dallas and Denver after it was promised tax breaks and incentives that could total $60 million over 20 years by the city of Chicago and the State of Illinois," as reported by the *New York Times* in 2001.[225] Seattle—which had been the airline maker's headquarters city for decades—lost Boeing, Chicago lost $60 million, and the American people gained nothing of value from this zero-sum game of musical chairs.

In California, State Controller John Chiang, speaking out in 2011 against profligate redevelopment agencies, had this to say: "For a government activity which consumes more than $5.5 billion of public resources annually, we should be troubled that there are no objective performance measures demonstrating that taxpayers are receiving optimal return for each invested dollar . . . ."[226] When auditors from the controller's office had conducted a review of 18 redevelopment agencies (RDAs) in fiscal year 2009–2010, they had found that the RDAs "share no consensus in defining a blighted area. While run-down sections of Los Angeles with abandoned buildings show obvious need for redevelopment, other cities were far broader in their declaration of blight. . . .. In Palm Desert, redevelopment dollars are being used to renovate greens and bunkers at a 4.5-star golf resort."[227]

After that revelation, it didn't take long for the State of California to react—first its legislature, then its courts. As reported in the *Los Angeles Times* of December 29, 2011, "The California Supreme Court . . . ruled unanimously in favor of a state law passed last summer that abolished redevelopment agencies . . .. More than 400 redevelopment agencies will cease to exist after Feb. 1. . . .. The ruling, written by Justice Kathryn Mickle Werdegar, said the Legislature had the power to create redevelopment agencies and the power to end them."[228]

Redevelopment abuse is rampant all across America because it is easy for unscrupulous developers to find ways to syphon off redevelopment funds to enrich themselves at the expense of the public good, and inept public officials often waste redevelopment funds on frills that do nothing to improve the local economy.

As a citizen activist, you need to keep an eye on your local redevelopment agency, looking for signs of corruption or government gullibility and credulity that allow officials and elected leaders to be easily tricked into such ill-advised courses of action as these:

- A project drags on and on, year after year, without results
- An "angel" investor promises to "be there" if something goes wrong—but has no legal obligation to do so and then fails to show up when needed
- A blowhard developer offers a "too good to be true" proposal— and such proposals usually are, with nasty results for the city
- Shoeless Joe Jackson promises, "If you build it, they will come."[229]

CITY OF SPRAWL

Shortly after moving to the spot on a map of California that I will call the city of Sprawl, I toured its downtown, taking notes and recording my impressions. I was stunned by the extent of dilapidation. The dilapidation didn't bother me that much; I've worked in some very run-down cities over the years. But what did bother me as a city planner were all the missed opportunities to make the city a better place to live.

Missed opportunities. To the eye of a city planner, downtown Sprawl is like a mass of modeling clay from which one of America's great urban centers could be built, but a lack of vision has turned that clay into hardpan. Ironically, the worst damage has been inflicted by the city itself. The city has compounded its blight by allowing new blight to be introduced in the form of incompatible, inappropriate, and low-quality infill development—that is, new construction on scattered vacant or underutilized land.

Urban redevelopment basics. Sprawl doesn't understand that before anyone builds a new structure in a redevelopment area, the proposal must comply with the basics we looked at a few pages back: it must have a vision, a theme, a work plan, and a timeline. If there are any local plans for Sprawl's many redevelopment projects that are in accord with those basics, they are well-kept secrets. None of the documents I was able to obtain under the California Public Records Act could be considered "plans" as commonly defined.

Seeing what I saw during my walk-around made me curious. Had any members of the city council ever explored their own downtown, closely and critically? Had any of them actually lived there? Had any of them ever *been* downtown? In a national magazine, I read an article that discussed how Sprawl's downtown might still look like a rat hole but that it was about to spring back to life because someone (perhaps a pixie) had made big, important decisions about redevelopment and was about to surprise everyone with a wonderland that would appear out of thin air.

I have met Sprawl's whole redevelopment crew: none of them is a pixie. So far, they've failed to revitalize Sprawl's downtown after 40 years of tinkering with this and that. I suspect the unwary magazine reporter was wined and dined by city hall's imaginative public relations department.

Failed redevelopment. Sprawl has as many as 26 partially completed redevelopment projects, some of which have languished for more than 40 years. The city is no closer to completing these moldering projects than it was 20 or 30 years ago. In fact, during the intervening four decades blight has gobbled up even more of Sprawl, creating a vast wasteland of vacant lots, collapsing buildings, and obsolete land uses. Sprawl's inability to act on its own redevelopment in a timely manner has left property owners in a jam. They are afraid to invest money in properties the redevelopment agency might take from them, and they can't sell because the threat of redevelopment scares away buyers.

During the eight years I lived in Sprawl, I saw city hall dance to the same tune over and over again:

1. An out-of-town developer presents a grand scheme to save the city's downtown. Some well-known companies offer to come to the rescue but then suddenly want a few dollars for their "free" help, then a few more, and on and on.
2. City hall gets all excited but never asks how a scheme will work. In one instance, city hall was talked into investing in a plan, only to find out that the promoter didn't own the land. (The actual out-of-state owner had no knowledge of the scheme.)
3. City hall is asked to fund a scheme and take all the risk, while the developer plans on raking in all of the profit without taking any risk.
4. City hall backs out, realizing they have been conned once again—after wasting a lot of time and losing a lot of money.

With a little common sense and ingenuity, Sprawl could have created a spectacular downtown, but it lacked both common-sense leadership and the technical expertise to know the difference between a workable proposal and a pipe dream. During the time I lived there I read countless articles in the local newspaper pleading for constructive action, but nothing ever came of it. Over the years Sprawl has had a city council that openly practiced "cronyism," with elected officials siphoning off government dollars to enrich themselves and their buddies. Recently the county district attorney set up a task force to track down evildoers. But that has been tried before, with no lasting improvement. I lived in Sprawl for more than eight years, and found it to be a pleasant city with great potential if it could only escape from its heritage of petty graft and corruption—the people of Sprawl deserve better.

Chapter 8
THE PRESERVATION PLAN

The difference between a preservation plan and a redevelopment plan is the way they are financed. Preservation work is funded by general obligation bonds, bake sales, raffles, or begging. Well, at least it *seems* that way. Without tax allocation bonds, as explained in the previous chapter, there's just not enough cash available to get rid of blight and rebuild with the highest and best land uses. So, preservation has to start by preserving the best properties in the best neighborhoods, and it has to do so without spending a lot of money.

WHAT IS PRESERVATION?

Preservation is the process of keeping something that is valued from falling into ruin. It means eliminating conditions that will eventually lead to blight, by restoring or refurbishing real estate in the area. It does *not* mean replacing existing neighborhood ambiance by "modernizing" or "upzoning" to a higher land-use density. Preservation does not replace a familiar place—such as an historic downtown—with an incongruous suburban shopping mall.

By definition, preservation is used to increase the value of a parcel of real estate by assuring that every property within a neighborhood will meet city code requirements when the preservation work is completed.

PRESERVATION AGENCY

A preservation plan should be written under the direction of a public agency set up by the city to specifically administer preservation. Trying to administer preservation by assigning tasks to employees from various city departments on an as-needed basis becomes too complicated to be effective. But that doesn't mean that a preservation agency shouldn't allow city departments to bid for work, the same as outside contractors. There just needs to be a clear chain of command and accountability.

A preservation agency, like a redevelopment agency, should operate as much like a free enterprise business as the law allows. Preservation, like redevelopment, is neither a social service agency nor a charity. A preservation agency is composed of three businesslike components—the same as a redevelopment agency:

Real estate broker. A preservation agency is a real estate brokerage business that may appraise, market, manage, exchange, and auction property, and also prepare contracts and leases.

Real estate developer. A preservation agency is a real estate development business that buys land and readies it for construction. The developer may employ design professionals and construction contractors, subdivide property, install infrastructure, and erect structures.

Real estate lender. A preservation agency is a real estate finance business that may provide short-term acquisition, development, and construction financing (AD&C) and lend money for renovation. It may acquire federal and state grants and pass subsidies on to the end users. The revolving loan fund is replenished when individual projects repay their loans.

VISION, THEME, WORK PLAN, TIMELINE

Preservation is used to increase the value of a parcel of real estate by assuring that every property within a neighborhood will meet city code requirements when the work is completed. Like redevelopment, preservation requires the proper application of technique based on the following four elements:

Vision. A preservation agency needs people in positions of responsibility who are able to visualize a finished project—a particular talent of design professionals.

Theme. Preservation should set an overall design theme and aim at creating a unique or recognizable setting for each neighborhood. This is done by remodeling existing buildings that detract from the overall theme or by adding public amenities that pull a theme together: trees, street signs, streetlights, sidewalks, and so on. The preservation agency may also help property owners choose appropriate paint colors and roofing materials—and maybe get rid of those pink flamingos and garden gnomes.

As a famous example of a neighborhood theme, San Francisco stands out as the city of the "Painted Ladies." Numerous Victorian and Edwardian-style houses built in the city between 1849 and 1915 were painted in bright colors, but during WWII many of them were painted battleship gray or stripped of their Victorian decor. Then in 1963, "San Francisco artist Butch Kardum began combining intense blues and greens on the exterior of his Italianate-style Victorian house. . . . . By the 1970s, this 'colorist movement' had changed entire streets and neighborhoods."[230]

The Painted Ladies near Alamo Square in San Francisco are some of the most photographed houses ever. Back in the 1940s, some of them were gray, stripped-down relics. Now they are revered. Many older neighborhoods all over America might benefit from the "colorist movement."

Work plan. An achievable plan must include detailed design specifications, precise costs, and a realistic marketing strategy. You need a property-by-property plan that everyone in the neighborhood can see and be able to evaluate and criticize, both privately and at public forums.

Timeline. A firm schedule is needed, showing the timeline of events from beginning to end. A preservation project, like redevelopment, should be finished within five years. As of 2018, the average length of home ownership in the U.S. was said to be 13.3 years.[231] So preservation needs to move right along, so that the original homeowners will still be around to see the final results.

"BOUGHT FOR A SONG"

In 2006 the Arizona city of Glendale enacted its Historic Preservation Element, which was supposed to guide downtown preservation. But nothing became of the preservation plan. When I walk around the downtown, I can see for myself that the plan failed because the city gave up—it didn't complete the restoration. As reported by John Barry for azfamily.com in 2018, "Business isn't exactly booming in downtown Glendale with a number of vacant shops and a lack of new development. So, you'd expect a lot of excitement surrounding the City's plan to sell an empty [building]. . .. Instead, the deal is under scrutiny after the City Council agreed to sell the property for $25,000. The City purchased the building in 2008 for $735,000. . .. 'We're granted the ability to do what is in the best interest of the City,' said [city manager Kevin] Phelps.[232]

Why do cities constantly want to "give away the store" by writing down city-owned property—it's a formula for failure. Don't do it!

PUBLIC NUISANCE LAWS, DEALING WITH OBSTACLES

Public nuisance laws are the "stick" a preservation agency has available if all else fails. But it's not what you want to use, because it creates enemies and makes property owners afraid of your preservation agency. It is always better to use persuasion, incentives (money), or peer pressure to get recalcitrant owners to fix up their property. Most people can be persuaded to comply by virtue of their need to be loved and to be part of the group. It's not much fun being an outcast.

While virtually every local government has the authority to enact a local public nuisance ordinance requiring property owners to maintain their real estate in good repair, using this "stick" is usually more trouble than it is worth. In many situations, your preservation agency will be better off ignoring the nuisance and going on with the rest of the work. Chances are the nuisance property will soon be sold or fixed up without further city action.

Winning over opponents. Preservation abuse is rampant all across America because many preservation agencies give up as soon as they encounter opposition or fail to do much to improve a neighborhood. I've seen many cities walk away from preservation plans because some vocal group showed up at city hall to oppose them. But in my experience, with a little extra work and inclusion of your opponents you can come up with a plan nearly everyone can endorse. Opponents are usually people who feel they've been left out of the planning and decision-making process.

Traditionalist neighborhoods. On the other hand, there are neighborhoods dominated by traditionalists who just want to be left alone. Such neighborhoods will most likely reject any city-sponsored preservation plan. It is often wiser to bypass these neighborhoods rather than force preservation onto them.

It turns out that traditionalists have a distinct outlook on life; they react with an exaggerated response when faced with something they perceive as threatening. A study in the journal *Science* found that traditionalists have a stronger physiological reaction to startling noises and graphic images than do other people. Another study published in *Current Biology* found that traditionalists tend to have a larger amygdala—a cerebral structure that is electrically active during states of fear and anxiety. And a third study found that self-identified traditionalists generate more brain activity overall in response to disturbing images.[233]

EXISTING INFRASTRUCTURE

Before you adopt a preservation plan, you need to evaluate the condition of your public infrastructure. How old is it, and what's the existing capacity?

Transportation and water are the major categories of public infrastructure, as reported by the Brookings Institution, and "water infrastructure, has . . . seen a drop in spending over the past decade. Spending on drinking water, wastewater, and other water resources like lakes and reservoirs makes up the remaining 32.2 percent of all U.S. infrastructure spending. Local water utilities, in particular, have struggled to keep up with pursuing needed capital projects alongside rising maintenance needs."[234]

Increased housing density. The Minneapolis City Council voted on October 25, 2019 to adopt the Minneapolis 2040 Comprehensive Plan which will allow up to three units on all single-family residential properties—trickle-down housing affordability? But according to Michael Storper, UCLA and London School of Economics professor, "The idea that upzoning will cause housing affordability to trickle down within our metropolis . . . is just a lot to promise—and it's based on a narrative of housing as opportunity that is deeply flawed. We have to be very cautious when we use a storyline like that to justify public policy."[235]

When a part of your city is subdivided into lots and houses are then constructed, the public infrastructure is sized to accommodate the total number of households. If at a later date the city increases the number of households in the area, the infrastructure will also need to be resized to service the added households. The Minneapolis City Council didn't seem to take that into consideration, or if they did, they chose to ignore it. Upzoning has many expensive hidden trappings that go along with the promise of easy money.

INFILL DEVELOPMENT

Infill development is defined as constructing new buildings in the vacant space between existing buildings. This usually takes place in run-down neighborhoods where the original development occurred a building at a time, without any overall plan. Often these neighborhoods were marketed as "ranchettes" and sold to families that valued junk cars and rusted-away farm equipment more than farm animals or suburban landscaping.

Over time these old-fashioned impromptu housing tracts have failed to reach full development because they are unsightly and often lack curbs, gutters, and sidewalks. Frequently the lots are served by individual water wells and septic tanks, with high incidents of contamination and failure. Run-down ranchette neighborhoods can be gold mines for preservation agencies. They can be upgraded by installing underground utilities, redividing oversized lots, and infilling with a variety of mixed development—multifamily housing, convenience shopping, and service commercial—such as medical offices or even light industrial development.

To bring a rundown, partially developed neighborhood up to today's standards, the preservation agency needs to use the planned unit development (PUD) process to tie the whole neighborhood together and create a sense of place. And yes, ranchettes, apartments, and corner stores can share the same neighborhood with good results—if done by talented design professionals. This also provides an opportunity to reintroduce the traditional architecture and landscaping of your "nation". This is where a team of form-based code experts can prove their value.

ALLEY RESTORATION

An alley may be defined as a garden walk bordered by trees or bushes. Or it may be defined as a narrow street running through the middle of a block, giving access to the rear of lots. Neighborhoods laid out on the gridiron street pattern usually orient the house to face the street and the garage to face the alley at the rear of the lot. In times past, houses were typically built with care, while the garages or horse barns facing the ally were typically flimsy, utilitarian structures. Over time, alleys have tended to fall into disrepair and end up as neighborhood nuisances. Sometimes they are all but abandoned, the garages torn down, and serve only for trash collection.

But run-down alleys can be profit centers for preservation agencies. Depending on the lot width, a new garage building with two to four stalls on the ground floor and one or two apartments on an upper story can easily be built facing the alley.

According to *Epic Home Ideas* online magazine, a standard two-car garage should be 20 feet deep with an interior width of 18 feet and a 16-foot double doorway. Standard four-car garage dimensions should be 22 feet deep, with 16-foot-wide double doorways and an interior width of 36 feet. [236] What these dimensions mean is that on a very narrow lot, about 25 feet in width, you can build a standard two-car garage with a 360-square-foot apartment upstairs, doubling the housing density on your lot and producing an income. On a wider lot of around 50 feet, you can build a standard four-car garage with two 396-square-foot apartments upstairs, tripling the housing density on your lot and producing even more income. I know of cities where thousands of over-the-garage apartments could be added to the housing stock. Of course, before adding extra housing facing an ally, your city would need to determine if the existing public utilities are adequate, or if they must be updated—replacing wires and pipes is expensive.

GENTRIFICATION

Gentrification is typically defined as a process in which a poor neighborhood experiences an influx of wealthier people who renovate homes and businesses, often resulting in an increase in property values and the displacement of poorer residents. Andrew Lee, writing in *Teen Vogue*, expresses views on gentrification that fail the test of objectivity, in my opinion.[237] One of those interviewed, "Daniel G., a lifelong resident of San Jose, California, . . . sees these profit-driven neighborhood expulsions as a form of colonialism, the latest chapter in a story that began with the mass kidnapping of Africans through chattel slavery and forced dispossession of the land of Indigenous peoples to build the United States."[238] Says a second interviewee, Liz Gonzalez of the non-profit South Bay Community Land Trust, "the places that get gentrified seem to be where people of color live. You just push 'em out, push 'em out."[239]

Lee goes on to say, "When Amazon wanted to build a new campus in Queens, New York, residents who feared being priced out mounted a successful campaign that contributed to stopping the development. In San Jose, some residents are fighting a proposed Google campus that could lead to the displacement of thousands, with some even blocking a Google bus carrying employees to work in 2018."[240]

What these people are missing is that the real problem is not about gentrification—it's education, income distribution, and the nature of work in the economy of the future. Gentrification itself is the *preservation* of neighborhoods, something that is beneficial to society. (I hope I didn't earn my master's degree in Urban and Regional Planning so I could save slum neighborhoods from being improved.) Rather than lashing out at gentrification, opponents could instead be paying attention to income inequality. According to the U.S. Census Bureau, average earnings in 2018 ranged from $18,900 for high school dropouts to $25,900 for high school graduates, $45,400 for college graduates, and $99,300 for workers with professional degrees." [241] People at the low end of the pay scale don't earn enough money to live comfortably anywhere in America.

UPZONING

Upzoning is defined as changing the zoning to allow taller or denser buildings. Upzoning usually involves revising the zoning of single-family residential lots to allow construction of multifamily dwellings such as duplexes, triplexes, or four-plexes.

According to the Urban Displacement Project of the University of California, Berkeley, "While upzoning may change market dynamics in some neighborhoods, in others, the existing stock or costs of construction may mean upzoning will do little to make new housing developments financially viable."[242] Perhaps Berkeley is saying that upzoning may make housing affordable in some neighborhoods, but in others the cost of construction may be so high that upzoning will do little to make new housing affordable. I can understand that.

Yonah Freemark, a doctoral student in urban planning at MIT, evaluated the impact of upzoning near transit stops in Chicago neighborhoods. Freemark found the following:

- Upzoning had no impact on housing supply.
- Housing prices rose on up zoned property.[243]

The Minneapolis 2040 Plan. As previously mentioned, the Minneapolis City Council voted in 2019 to approve its 2040 Comprehensive Plan. The plan went into effect on January 1, 2020. Initial zoning changes allow up to three units on all residential properties and require a percentage of affordable housing units in new apartment buildings. Jenny Schetz of the Brookings Institution has written about the Minneapolis 2040 plan. Below are her observations and my rebuttals to those observations:[244]

- **Build more housing.** "By rezoning lots that currently accommodate only one single-family house to allow duplexes and triplexes, Minneapolis effectively triples the housing capacity of some neighborhoods."

    Rebuttal. Single-family dwellings aren't designed to be cut up into triplexes. The remodeling process is expensive and includes installing individual electric meters and replumbing to accommodate more water taps, and sewer lines. Unless, of course, the triplex is to be a tenement house that only meets minimum standards for sanitation, safety, and comfort. Chopped-up houses rarely possess any charm or aesthetic value because the original coherent design rarely survives the remodeling.

- **Build less expensive housing**. "A 3,000-square-foot structure divided into three apartments not only creates more housing units, but each apartment will be cheaper than the single-family house it replaces. [Developers will not have to] . . . provide off-street parking for new houses. . ..”

Rebuttal. The average size of a new American house is 2,349 square feet. Realistically there are few 3,000-square-foot single-family houses. When I browsed Zillow, I found a few in the $1 million price bracket—not likely candidates for chopping up into triplexes. And even if a real estate developer was looking for houses to chop up, I doubt they would triple the housing capacity of any neighborhood. I’ve never seen upzoning convert more than a sprinkling of single-family homes in any one neighborhood—just enough to spoil the existing milieu.

- **Build less-expensive housing in desirable neighborhoods.** “The [plan will improve] affordability in high amenity neighborhoods. Key features of those neighborhoods are proximity to employment centers, public transit stations, low crime, low poverty, and high-quality public schools.”

Rebuttal. If upzoning brings duplexes and triplexes to a high-amenity neighborhood, the people who make the neighborhood “high amenity” will quietly move away, taking their low crime, low poverty, and high-quality public schools with them. I’ve seen this happen time and time again.

One last question. After Minneapolis sacrifices the integrity of every single-family neighborhood, I wonder by how many dollars the incomes of poor households will have been increased? The United States—the world’s largest economy with a nominal GDP of $21.44

trillion, constituting a quarter of the world economy[245]—needs to end its highly unequal distribution of wealth. The wealthiest 1 percent of families in the U.S. hold about 40 percent of all wealth, according to the Washington Center for Equitable Growth, while the bottom 90 percent hold less than a quarter of the wealth.[246]

COMPLETE STREETS

The design approach called "Complete Streets" requires that streets to be planned, designed, and maintained for safe travel and access for users regardless of their mode of transportation.

Complete Streets emphasizes the importance of safe access for all users—whether walking, cycling, driving, riding public transportation, or delivering goods—and not just for automobiles.[320]

Reconfiguring your city's streets to these standards may require expensive repaving, moving curbs, widening sidewalks, and narrowing traffic lanes. But the cost may soon be repaid in lower accident rates, a heightened sense of place, and increased property values. The improved aesthetics—landscaping and street furniture—will also increase the overall attractiveness of your city.

TIDY TOWNS

The idea behind Ireland's annual Tidy Towns contest is to encourage communities to see themselves the way strangers might see them. Tidy Towns is also about doing things properly—good planning, well-maintained buildings and public spaces, appropriate landscaping and respect for natural amenities [the physical characteristics that enhance the location as a place to live].

Eight criteria are assessed:

- Community involvement and planning

- Built environment and streetscape
- Landscaping and open spaces
- Wildlife, habitats, and natural amenities
- Tidiness and litter control
- Sustainable waste and resource management
- Residential streets and housing areas
- Approach roads, streets, and lanes[247]

The Tidy Towns contest could be applied to the neighborhoods in *your* city—give it a try. Good luck—*go n-éirí an t-ádh libh*!

Chapter 9
YOU CAN MAKE A DIFFERENCE

In the classic 1946 Christmas film *It's a Wonderful Life*, Bedford Falls and Pottersville are the same city—only the planning is different.[248] Pottersville is the sleazy town that Bedford Falls would have become without the actions of George Bailey (James Stewart) over the years. Likewise, there are two visions of *your* city—your own and Mr. Potter's. If you don't take part in the planning, Mr. Potter will do it for you.

If you want to get involved in local planning, I suggest you read my book *Fight City Hall and Win: How to Defend Your Community Against Rapacious Developers, Scared Bureaucrats, and Corrupt Politicians*. My book gives citizen activists detailed instructions on how local government operates and how to participate in decision-making—it's a do it yourself book that works.

LOCAL PLANS—LONGING FOR HOME

In 2005, Portland, Oregon Mayor Tom Potter initiated a public engagement process to uncover the underlying values that create urban livability in Portland, Oregon.[249] It was found that Portlanders understood that livability, or quality of life, is created by "conscious intent" rather than by chance. They reached general agreement on ten quality-of-life issues:

- A clean and beautiful environment, both natural and built
- Vibrant, well-served neighborhoods
- Access to green space and nature, within the city and around it
- The ability to get around town easily (lack of traffic, accessible public transportation, ability to bike and use alternate modes, relatively short commute times)
- Human scale and human-oriented buildings and streets (not too big, walkable blocks, user-centered design)
- Big-city amenities with a small-town feel
- Friendly and open-minded people who care about the environment, education, and a host of social issues
- A thriving local economy providing access to fresh local food, local beer, coffee, clothing design, local musicians and art
- Affordability for living in and enjoying the city
- A sense of community fostered by public spaces, neighborhoods, walking and using public transit, outdoor events, and the local economy.[250]

Portland's 2005 discovery process looks to me like a good way to start upgrading America's urban livability. We should by now have learned that the "growth at all cost" and "bigger is better" approach does not work. Neither does "endless sprawl and a mall."

MALLING THE HEART OF DOWNTOWN

In 1952 the magazine *Progressive Architecture* ran an article by Vienna-born architect Victor Gruen. that put forth his belief—as detailed in a 2012 article for Bloomberg CityLab—that "by locating all of a community's shopping needs in an enclosed mall, with a nondescript exterior, we could do away with the 'commercial blight' of scattered hot-dog stands and gas stations and neon storefronts that made America, in his eyes, so ugly."[251]

Gruen thought he was creating better downtowns in the suburbs. He thought his malls would become civic centers with shopping, government offices, and community halls. He thought malls would function as public squares, like the traditional town squares of Europe. Incredibly, he didn't understand that adding all this new commercial space in the suburbs was taking business away from traditional downtowns. The first fully enclosed, climate-controlled mall—Southdale Center in Edina, Minnesota, a suburb of Minneapolis—opened in 1956. The day it opened, some 75,000 shoppers rushed in, but Gruen never figured out that these shoppers were also deserting Edina's downtown and that his malls would bankrupt downtown areas.

From 1956 through the 1990s, Gruen's enclosed-mall concept seemed to work quite well; by 1990 America was opening nineteen malls a year. Then consumer tastes changed, and mall building came to an abrupt end; no one has built a new enclosed mall since 2006.[252] Now about a third of all malls in the U.S. are dead or dying. A few years ago, I took a look at a once-thriving mall in Southern California and found that out of 200 stores, only fifteen were still hanging on—and not one of them was a money-making chain store. Once the chain stores leave, the Grim Reaper is not far behind.

UNMALLING DOWNTOWN

The following is a summation of the experience of Mountain View, California, and its farsighted city attorney, manager, redevelopment director, Bruce Liedstrand, as reported in the article "How Mountain View Revived Its Downtown."[253] The rise of shopping malls in the

1960s prompted Mountain View to try to revitalize their downtown. In an early attempt, a twelve-story office building was started, but it ended up uncompleted and sat empty for ten years. Following that misstep, a consultant was hired to prepare a plan, but that was also a disaster—the community rebelled. So, the city rounded up a group of citizen activists and charged them with coming up with a plan that would satisfy local needs.

Right off the bat, the group realized they didn't understand the ingredients needed for success, so they read about good downtowns, visited other downtowns, and talked with people about what they liked and didn't like about their existing downtown. Through their surveys, they learned that a downtown was a place for people to interact, not just a place to shop. They found that many cities thought it important to have a plan. But the citizen-activist group decided that what they really needed was a dream, and that cities that wrote their plans without dreams failed to change their downtowns into great places to work and live. They first needed to have a dream, and then to write a plan to turn that dream into reality.

They also found that a successful downtown needed to be compact and walkable. You expect to park your car only once during your visit. They also realized that placing a parking lot between a sidewalk and the stores puts an end to window-shopping, a pastime that connects pedestrians with businesses and is part of the overall downtown experience. In a traditional downtown—with its mix of retail on the ground floor and offices and residences on upper floors, surrounded by homes within walking distance—people spend a lot of time just walking around and enjoying the sights. And by the way, downtown buildings need to be at least two or three stories tall. Single-story buildings spoil the all-important "canyon" effect that's achieved when pedestrians look up and see human activity taking place above street level.

Another important observation was that home, work, and shopping needed to be comfortably mixed. A traditional downtown needs to feel like an open-air community living room; it's where the community holds the Fourth of July and Easter parades, where Santa lands with his sleigh. It's where friends and neighbors get together to socialize, and where people stop by for coffee or a treat.

The citizen group had to resist the advances of ostensibly all-knowing outside design professionals and developers who admonished that they were better equipped to come up with a correct project for downtown if the city would just relax its standards a little and accept "what the market wants and needs." These "experts" put pressure on the group to put more parking in front of new retail businesses because "that's how modern retail business functions." The Mountain View citizen activists would, I'm sure, have warned the rest of us, "Don't be tempted, or you'll destroy your dream. Stick with tried-and-true traditional downtown development standards, and watch your dream unfold as a downtown area that is successful and human scale."

CITIZEN INVOLVEMENT . . . OR SO THEY SAY

The US Environmental Protection Agency warns, "The first step in planning for public participation is to ensure that you are seeking to obtain and use public input and not merely seeking public buy-in to an already determined outcome."[254] The following exercise in citizen participation illustrates a situation where city hall is, in fact, seeking "public buy-in to an already determined outcome."[255]

Every few years, city halls across the nation send out announcements urging citizens to participate in some sort of local plan review. If you're considering going to city hall to participate in drafting fresh ideas that you've been told will be considered for inclusion in the new plan, there are some things you should know ahead of time. When you get to the venue, you'll notice that the auditorium walls are covered with professional sketches, maps, and charts that obviously took a lot of time to prepare. Soon you'll realize that you are coming into a process that has been underway for a long time. It's like showing up after the movie has started; it leaves you with the uncomfortable feeling that everyone around you knows the plot and you don't.

Charrette or charade? What you are about to experience is a charrette, or so you will be told.

- *Charrette*: a meeting in which stakeholders attempt to resolve conflicts and map out solutions
- *Charade*: something done under a pretense of being true when it actually is not.

Which will it be? Keep your eyes open, because the charrette you've been invited to will likely turn out to be a charade. The charrette is a favorite tool (or weapon) of design professionals who use it not as a vehicle for collaboration but as a mechanism of control. They already know what they want in their plan; you are there to support them, not to spoil the predetermined outcome.

The local plan-formulation charrette is a lengthy affair in which the audience is told that everyone there is going to work together to devise a new plan. The exercise may go on for as long as one or two weekends. If you show up to participate, you'll find yourself surrounded by an eclectic mob of the idle curious but also self-serving public officials, developers, and opportunists, all to be whirled and twirled by a smooth team of design professionals.

Accept the predetermined. A "successful" charrette (for the design professionals, that is) will be one in which the team of design pros deftly moves the audience along to where they accept the prearranged outcome. Dissent is neither invited nor tolerated. The typical response to dissent is "Thank you for sharing. Next question." One tipoff is the quickness with which the plan' illustrations show up to be posted on the walls for participants to admire. The preferred plan doesn't just appear out of nowhere. You can be darn sure a member of the local power structure will have let the design professionals know just what needs to be in the plan.

Charrette participants are usually dispersed to form themselves into small groups that look representative of the local community but rarely have the moral authority to represent the whole community. And always be aware that some participants will be there as part of a prearranged plan to promote someone's hidden agenda. Often, they are subcontractors, family members, or employees who want to keep their jobs.

In his bestseller *What Money Can't Buy*, Michael J. Sandel takes up one of the biggest ethical questions of our time: Isn't there something wrong with a world in which everything is for sale? If so, how can we prevent market values from reaching into spheres of life where they don't belong? In recent decades, market values have crowded out non-market norms in almost every aspect of life. Without quite realizing it, Sandel argues, we have drifted away from having a market economy to being a market society.[256]

Years ago, I was invited to participate in a charrette where, I was told, neighborhood people would be encouraged to work as a group to design a reuse plan for ten acres of surplus school property. Soon it became obvious that city hall wanted to convert the vacant school site into a transit mall to serve an adjoining shopping center, with some senior citizen housing thrown in to make it look legitimate—but the proposal violated the adopted general plan. City hall, in partnership with a favored developer, wanted to garner neighborhood support for the proposal, so they packed the audience with city transit employees and the developer's workers, friends, family, and subcontractors. I was one of a handful of actual neighborhood residents in attendance.

When I attempted to read several legal points into the public record, the chair (the head of the transit agency) reached over, unplugged my microphone, and told me my time was up. Then a chorus of bused-in stooges chanted for me to "shut up and go home." Someone asked for my written comments so they could be placed in the public record—and they were never seen again. Luckily, the proposal was so obviously a product of political corruption that city hall quietly ditched the scheme once the local newspaper got hold of it.

If you do go to a charrette, think of it as entertainment, not as a meaningful chance to add to the planning process. But don't despair, there's a way for you to really participate.

A FEW BASIC GROUND RULES

Planning is about the future—not the past and not even the present.

A plan needs to be written so that it will be understood by an audience that reads at the eighth-grade level.

- A plan must not be longer than 100 pages—not a single page more!
- A plan must be based on authentic citizen participation—no charades.
- A plan must address one of the four planning levels outlined in this book—general, limited, specific, or emergency.

- A plan must be something that can actually be implemented—
no magical thinking.

POPULATION STABILITY IS COMING

A successful city plan also needs to take into consideration the demographic changes that are likely to take place in the years ahead—in the city itself or even on a wider scale.

Population trends. As I said earlier in this book, the United States is expected to achieve its maximum population of about 364 million by the year 2062. Then population will decline to about 336 million by the year 2100.[257] Ten states have already reached zero population growth.

Just 40 years from now (two generations), city planners may be looking at ways to get rid of empty buildings and eliminate the over-supply of housing. Now is not the time to get hysterical about endless growth and urban sprawl.

The following population projections are from the Pew Research and the U.S. Census Bureau, along with my wild guess for 2080:

2020–2040. Population will grow to about 360 million (U.S. Census).

2040–2060. Population will grow to about 364 million (Pew Research).

2060–2080. Population will drop to about 350 million (My guess).

2080–2100. Population will decline to about 336 million (Pew Research).

By the time America might want to increase immigration in order to add population, there may not be many people who will want to leave their homelands. By 2100 some 90 countries are expected to lose population.[258] Immigration to the U.S. from Mexico has already declined—Mexico is becoming a country of older people with a $2.4 trillion economy, the eleventh-largest in the world as of 2018.[259] And Mexico ranks second highest in the Happy Planet Index results. Well-being in Mexico is rated higher than in the neighboring USA.[260] Why move north?

"BUY LAND, THEY'RE NOT MAKING IT ANYMORE" – MARK TWAIN.

The United States covers about 2.3 billion acres. In 2012, the United States Department of Agriculture estimated urbanization covered 70 million acres or 3 percent of the land."[261]

America has plenty of non-urban land available for future population growth. For example, "an average 16.7% of large US cities' land area is considered vacant."[262]

Dusty Ferguson, tells us in "These Places in the US Are Giving Out FREE Land in 2020," that many small cities in the Midwest are giving away buildable lots, just for the asking.[263]

And then there are those 3,800 ghost towns where nobody lives anymore. I don't suppose anyone would mind if you moved to one of them.

All we need is just a fraction of one percent of our total land area to provide places for America's projected maximum population to live.[264]

And don't forget that by the year 2062, our country will have reached a maximum population of about 364 million. After that the population will decline to about 336 million. Currently, the population is about 331 million. In the long run, another 5 million people isn't going to use up all that land where the buffalo roam and the deer and the antelope play.

The megacity fixation. The planning profession has historically concentrated on planning for bigger and bigger cities. Planners like to fantasize about planning for the most populated metropolitan areas in America: New York–Newark (18,351,295) or Los Angeles–Long Beach–Santa Ana (12,150,996). When mainstream planners show me their pictures of future cities, they all look about the same—mile-high skyscrapers, concrete desertscapes, and flying cars. At the same time, mainstream planning has pretty much ignored smaller human settlements. So, while much is written about megacities, little time is spent on smaller, more out-of-the-way places.

Unnoticed by mainstream planning, according to Adam McCann on the website WalletHub,[265] the fastest-growing places in America are Fort Myers, Florida; Bend, Oregon; Meridian, Idaho; Milpitas, California; and Enterprise, Nevada. *U.S. News & World Report* lists these as the fastest-growing places in 2020–2021: Myrtle Beach, South Carolina; Fort Myers, Florida; Naples, Florida; Sarasota, Florida; and Ocala, Florida.[266] These aren't places that attract the big employers—they are the "nice places" where people go to retire or work on their own. If you're planning to work from home, these are cities worth looking at.

Working from home. Stanford professor Nicholas Bloom conducted a two-year study of employees at China's biggest travel agency.[267] The study divided 500 employees into two groups: a control group who continued working at headquarters and a group who worked from home. Bloom found an astounding productivity boost among the work-from-home group:

- They worked a full day.
- They found it less distracting and easier to concentrate at home.

- They took shorter breaks, had fewer sick days, and took less time off.

Bloom's study indicates that working at home may be feasible in many situations. But because the study was conducted in China, with only a small sample of people working for a single company, the study is not statistically valid. More studies need to be conducted to confirm the results.

However, Bloom's study also found that more than half of the work-from-home group felt isolated after a while and wanted to work part time at headquarters and part time from home. Human contact is important—remember the study in which monkeys able to play with other monkeys, even for brief periods during their isolation, developed into healthy adults—human contact—seems to be essential to us primates.[268]

But in America, where 27 percent of the population says they want to live in a rural area, people may need to work at home without frequent office contact. What works or does not work in the short range may very well work in the long run.

Shared workspace. Rather than work at headquarters or at home, many people are opting for shared workspaces.

One provider, WeWork says: "With over 800 locations worldwide, WeWork offers you workspace where and how you need it, whether your goal is to be closer to home, empower your team in different cities, or have a go-to private space where you can actually focus."[269]

Many startups, freelances and gig workers have found shared workspace to be a cost-effective solution—I've been using shared office space, off and on, since the 1980s. Shared office space gives me a fixed business address, a receptionist, access to office machines, and way back when, a telephone answering service.

Shared office space also gives us work at home folks a place to go in the morning and a place where we can interact (act out) with unrelated primates, rather than bother our family members.

Based on my own experience, I suspect the shared workspace concept will become much more common because it provides a hideaway close to your home, and the all-important human contact we all need. I've always been able to find office space within walking or cycling distance from my home. Even in Alaska I found nearby office space.

REAL CITIZEN INVOLVEMENT

If you want your community to be a "nice" place to live, you have to adopt rules and regulations that lead to "nice," and you have to enforce them. You may find that sometimes you are the only person willing to defend your community from those who abide only by the rules of self-interest.

In 1947, the *San Francisco Chronicle* ran this headline: "Mayor Roger Lapham proclaimed, 'Junk the cable cars!'"[270] In response, resident Friedel Klussmann founded the Citizens' Committee to Save the Cable Cars. Her committee placed an amendment on the November ballot that year and it passed by a landslide. San Franciscans rallied to save the city's cable cars.

Sometimes it only takes one person. That person could be you.

City planning theory tells us that the purpose of long-range urban planning is to set aside the most appropriate locations for the placement of future land uses for the city and its inhabitants. Powerbrokers use long-range planning to position their land holdings so they will become the most profitable locations for *them*. You, as an active citizen, are the only one who can keep long-range planning from degenerating into just another way for the self-interested to prevail at society's expense.

ENDNOTES

Chapter 1: Introduction to City Planning

1. https://www.google.com/search?rlz=1C1CHBF_enUS927US927&-source=univ&tbm=isch&q=cities+of+the+future&sa=X&ved=2a-hUKEwjEtf6F5-zvAhXMPn0KHeAuBTAQjJkEegQIHx-AB&cshid=1617821747052400&biw=1900&bih=896

2. Frank Newport, "Americans Big on Idea of Living in the Country," Gallup, 07 DEC 2018, https://news.gallup.com/poll/245249/americans-big-idea-living-country.aspx

3. Charlotte O'Malley 80 Percent of Americans Prefer Single-Family Homeownership," Builder, "13 AUG 2013

4. Philip Reynolds, The Biblical Definitions Of The Pursuit Of Happiness, HuffPost, 25MAY2011, https://www.huffpost.com/entry/the-pursuit-of-what_b_781092

5. House Bill 2001: More Housing Choices for Oregonians, State of Oregon, https://www.oregon.gov/lcd/UP/Documents/HB2001OverviewPublic.pdf

6. "Minneapolis 2040 Plan," Local Housing Solutions, 2020, https://www.localhousingsolutions.org/plan/case-study-library/minneapolis-2040-plan/

7. "Resource-rich neighborhoods – affordable housing in," LocalHousingSolutions.org, https://www.localhousingsolutions.org/affordable-housing-in-opportunity-areas-or-resource-rich-neighborhoods/

8. Jessica Semega, Melissa Kollar, Emily A. Shrider, and John Creamer, "Income and Poverty in the United States 2019: Report Number P60-270," U.S. Census Bureau, 15SEP2020, https://www.census.gov/library/publications/2020/demo/p60-270.html

9. James Brasuell, "Berkeley to Remove Parking Requirements for Residential Properties," Planetizen, 27 JAN 2021, https://www.

planetizen.com/news/2021/01/112016-berkeley-remove-parking-require-ments-residential-properties

10. The Rise of the Anti-Car Movement, Finance Geek, https://www.finance-geek.org/politics/rise-of-anti-car-movement/

11. s.e. smith, "Why I Started Attending City Council Meetings," Bustle, 29 DEC 2015, https://www.bustle.com/articles/130400-why-i-started-at-tending-city-council-meetings

12. St. Augustine, Florida, Wikipedia, https://en.wikipedia.org/wiki/St._Augustine,_Florida

13. "Roanoke Colony" Wikipedia, https://en.wikipedia.org/wiki/Roanoke_Colony

14. Ibid

15. "Cahokia," Wikipedia, https://en.wikipedia.org/wiki/Cahokia

16. "Chaco Culture National Historical Park," Wikipedia, https://en.wikipe-dia.org/wiki/Chaco_Culture_National_Historical_Park

17. "10 oldest cities in the world," EducationWorld, Mumbai, https://www.educationworld.in/10-oldest-cities-in-the-world/

18. "Standard State Zoning Enabling Act and Standard City Planning Enabling Act," American Planning Association, Chicago, https://www.planning.org/growingsmart/enablingacts/

19. Ibid.

20. "A city planning primer," United States Department of Commerce. Advisory Committee on Zoning, Washington, D.C., 1928

21. Ibid.

22. Ibid

23. Ibid

24. Ibid

25. Ibid

26. Ibid

27. "Basic Needs Law and Legal Definition", USLegal, https://definitions.uslegal.com/b/basic-needs/#:~:text=Basic%20needs%20consists%20of%20adequate,%2C%20sanitation%2C%20health%20and%20educa-tion.

28. Crispin Jenkinson, "Quality of life," Encyclopedia Britannica, Inc., https://www.britannica.com/topic/quality-of-life

29. "7th Generation Principle," Seven Generations International, http://7gen-foundation.org/7th-generation/

30. "Seven generation sustainability," Wikipedia, https://en.wikipedia.org/wiki/Seven_generation_sustainability

31. "California Government Code - Section 65450-65457: Article 8. Specific Plans"

32. Local Assistance, St. Louis District Office, "How to Write a Business Plan," SBA.gov, https://www.sba.gov/offices/district/mo/st-louis/resources/how-write-business-plan

33.   Bankruptcy Statistics, ABI, https://www.abi.org/newsroom/bankrupt-cy-statistics, May 2, 2020

34.   https://www.google.com/search?q=number+of+ghost-towns+in+usa&rlz=1C1CHBF_enUS829US829&oq=number+of+ghost-towns+in+usa&aqs=chrome...69i57j0l2.17327j1j7&sourceid=-chrome&ie=UTF-8, May 2, 2020

35.   Tracking made easy, Universal-Information, https://universal-info.com/press-clippings/

36.   GreenBiz, https://www.greenbiz.com/

37.   "SBA Recommended Business Plans & Length," Small Business Administration, https://www.sba.gov/offices/district/az/phoenix/resources/sba-recommended-business-plans-length.

38.   Literacy in the United States, Wikipedia, https://en.wikipedia.org/wiki/Literacy_in_the_United_States

39.   Valerie Strauss, Reporter, "Hiding in plain sight: The adult literacy crisis", The Washington Post, 01NOV2016 https://www.washingtonpost.com/news/answer-sheet/wp/2016/11/01/hiding-in-plain-sight-the-adult-litera-cy-crisis/

40.   Martin Lind, "What the Heck is Plain Language," Granicus, https://granicus.com/blog/what-the-heck-is-plain-language/

41.   Natalie Wexler, "Why Americans can't write," The Washington Post, 24SEP2015, https://www.washingtonpost.com/opinions/why-americans-cant-write/2015/09/24/6e7f420a-6088-11e5-9757-e49273f05f65_story.html

42.   "Office of the Director of National Intelligence," https://www.dni.gov/index.php/plain-language-act

43.   "How Urban Planning Works", HowStuffWorks, https://science.howstuff-works.com/environmental/green-science/urban-planning.htm

44.   Anthony Cilluffo and Neil G. Ruiz, "World's population is projected to nearly stop growing by the end of the century," Pew Research Center, 17 JUN 2019, https://www.pewresearch.org/fact-tank/2019/06/17/worlds-population-is-projected-to-nearly-stop-growing-by-the-end-of-the-cen-tury/

45.   Sabine Balk, Demographic Trends: Differentiated Action, DandC, 22 JAN 2015, https://www.dandc.eu/en/article/study-illuminates-reasons-sustained-high-birth-rates-sub-saharan-africa

46.   Doyle Rice, "US, world population to shrink after midcentury, study suggests," USA Today, 14 JUL 2020, https://www.usatoday.com/story/news/nation/2020/07/14/lancet-study-us-world-population-shrink-af-ter-midcentury/5434571002/

47.   Ibid

Chapter 2: The General Plan

48. Jamie Munks, "Memphis City Council OKs South Cordova de-annexation," Memphis Commercial Appeal, 19 FEB 2019, https://www.commercialappeal.com/story/news/2019/02/19/two-square-miles-south-cordova-leave-city-memphis/2919591002/

49. "Petaluma Marks 30 Years of Growth Control," California Planning & Development Report, Initiatives and referendums, Local Watch, Paul Shigley, Sonoma County, Vol. 17 No. 04 APR 2002 01 APR 2002, https

50. Wendell Cox, "America Is More Small Town than We Think," NewGeography, 10 SEP 2008, https://www.newgeography.com/content/00242-america-more-small-town-we-think

51. Ibid

52. Ibid

53. Ibid

54. Ibid.

55. Wall Street Survivor Team (author), "Mcdonald's Real Estate: How They Really Make Their Money," Wall Street Survivor, 08 OCT 2015, https://blog.wallstreetsurvivor.com/2015/10/08/mcdonalds-beyond-the-burger/

56. Mark Funkhouser, "The Real Purpose of Government," Governing, OCT 2015, https://www.governing.com/gov-institute/on-leadership/gov-government-purpose-capitalism.html

57. "Timeline of human prehistory," Wikipedia, https://en.wikipedia.org/wiki/Timeline_of_human_prehistory

58. Lauren Coleman-Lochner and Jeremy Hill, "Hospital Bankruptcies Leave Sick and Injured Nowhere to Go," Bloomberg, 09JAN2020, https://www.bloomberg.com/news/articles/2020-01-09/hospital-bankruptcies-leave-sick-and-injured-nowhere-to-go

59. Dan O'Brien, "GM Closed the Lordstown Auto Plant. Now Ohio May Force a $60 Million Repayment." The Business Journal, 15 June 2020, https://www.propublica.org/article/gm-closed-the-lordstown-auto-plant-now-ohio-may-force-a-60-million-repayment

60. Ibid

61. Rick Paulas, "Sports Stadiums Are a Bad Deal for Cities But Cities Can Fight Back," the Atlantic, 21NOV2018, https://www.theatlantic.com/technology/archive/2018/11/sports-stadiums-can-be-bad-cities/576334/

62. Ovidijus Jurevicius, "Competitive advantage," Strategic Management Insight, 26SEP2013, https://strategicmanagementinsight.com/topics/competitive-advantage.html

63. Steve Olenski, "How To Rebrand A City," Forbs, 23OCT2017, https://www.forbes.com/sites/steveolenski/2017/10/23/how-to-rebrand-a-city/#6b66d2ac3bdf

64. "The Interview," Wikipedia, 2014, https://en.wikipedia.org/wiki/The_Interview

65. Steve Olenski, "How To Rebrand A City," Forbes, 23 OCT 2017, https://www.forbes.com/sites/steveolenski/2017/10/23/how-to-rebrand-a-city/?sh=326615c03bdf

66. "Occupational Outlook Handbook," Bureau of Labor Statistics, https://www.bls.gov/ooh/

67. Ibid

68. "Everything You Need to Know about Wind Turbine Technicians," Office of Energy Efficiency & Renewable Energy, 23OCT2017, https://www.energy.gov/eere/articles/everything-you-need-know-about-wind-turbine-technicians

69. "Fastest growing occupations," Table 1.3 Fastest growing occupations, 2018 and projected 2028 Bureau of Labor Statistics, https://www.bls.gov/emp/tables/fastest-growing-occupations.htm

70. Siôn Phillpott, "15 Disappearing Jobs that Won't Exist in 2030," Career Addict, 07JUL2020, https://www.careeraddict.com/disappearing-jobs

71. "California Government Code section 65300"

72. Harold Bartholomew, "Land Uses in American Cities," Harvard City Planning Studies 15 (Cambridge, MA: Harvard University Press, 1955).

73. "LV Strip (Nevada gaming area)," Wikipedia,

74. Allison Schrager, "Most Americans Are Single, and They're Changing the Economy," Bloomberg, September 12, 2014, http://www.bloomberg.com/bw/articles/2014-09-12/most-americans-are-single-dot-what-does-it-mean-for-the-economy.

75. "Standards for Outdoor Recreational Areas," Planning Advisory Service's report, American Planning Association, https://www.planning.org/pas/reports/report194.htm

76. John Moeller, "Standards for Outdoor Recreational Areas," Information Report No. 194, January 1965, American Society of Planning Officials, https://www.planning.org/pas/at60/report194.htm.

77. Ibid.

78. Jen Fifield, "Here's why the skies around Luke Air Force Base are getting noisier," The Republic, 05FEB2019, https://www.azcentral.com/story/news/local/glendale/2019/02/05/glendale-arizona-luke-air-force-base-f-35-program-grows-noise-grows/2778033002/

79. Carl Nolte, Chronicle Staff Writer, "Sprawl, Clutter Define Fresno / Civic corruption has splotched the city's image," SF Gate, 01 SEP 1999, https://www.sfgate.com/news/article/Sprawl-Clutter-Define-Fresno-Civic-corruption-2911067.php

80. How Many Miles Can a Truck Driver Drive in a Day? https://www.survivaltechshop.com/how-many-miles-can-a-truck-driver-drive-in-a-day/

81. Tony Arevalo, "24 Alarming Truck Accident Statistics for 2020," Carsurance, 10 APR 2020, https://carsurance.net/blog/truck-accident-statistics/

82. Brittany Chang, "This company is building the world's first network of self-driving delivery trucks across the US by 2024," Business Insider,

20JUL2020, https://www.businessinsider.com/tusimple-building-network-of-self-driving-delivery-trucks-us-2024-2020-7

83. "Autonomous Ship Project, Key Facts about Yara," Kongsberg Maritime, https://www.kongsberg.com/maritime/support/themes/autonomous-ship-project-key-facts-about-yara-birkeland/

84. "Life Cycle of a Ship," shippipedia, http://www.shippipedia.com/life-cycle-of-a-ship/

85. Bernard Marr, "The Incredible Autonomous Ships Of The Future: Run By Artificial Intelligence Rather Than A Crew." Forbs, 05 JUN 2019, https://www.forbes.com/sites/bernardmarr/2019/06/05/the-incredible-autonomous-ships-of-the-future-run-by-artificial-intelligence-rather-than-a-crew/#7c6cd33d6fbf

86. "Global Autonomous Trains Market Report (2020 to 2030) - COVID-19 Growth and Change," Research and Markets, 05 JUN 2020, https://www.prnewswire.com/news-releases/global-autonomous-trains-market-report-2020-to-2030---covid-19-growth-and-change-301071370.html

87. "Autonomous Trains on Long-distance." Future Markets Magazine, https://future-markets-magazine.com/en/markets-technology-en/autonomous-trains/

88. "Rio Tinto operates first driverless freight train," Railway Age, 16 JUL 2018, https://www.railwayage.com/freight/rio-tinto-operates-first-driverless-freight-train/

89. Brian McKenzie, "Who Drives to Work? Commuting by Automobile in the United States: 2013," U.S. Census Bureau, AUG 2015

90. "National Transit Database, 2017 National Transit Summary and Trends," Office of Budget and Policy, Federal Transit Administration, U.S. Department of Transportation, October 2018

91. Ridesharing company, Wikipedia

92. "A robot wrote this entire article. Are you scared yet, human," Guardian News & Media Limited, https://www.theguardian.com/commentis-free/2020/sep/08/robot-wrote-this-article-gpt-3

93. "Magnetic Elevators are Here and They're Not For the Fainthearted," The Future of Things (TFOT), https://thefutureofthings.com/11485-magnetic-elevators-theyre-not-fainthearted/

94. Ibid

95. Chris Giarratana, "Here's how self-driving cars could impact your city's planning," readwrite, 29 AUG 2017, https://readwrite.com/2017/08/29/self-driving-cars-city-planning-cl1/

96. Ibid

97. CityLift Automated Parking Systems

98. "Automated parking systems are cost-effective, versatile and space-saving," fata automation,14 FEB 2018, https://www.youtube.com/watch?v=VwS1QwXqgpk

99. https://www.abs.gov.au/AUSSTATS/abs@.nsf/mediareleasesbyRelease-Date/7DD5DC715B608612CA2581BF001F8404

100. Jonathan Lambert, "Greener Childhood Associated With Happier Adulthood," NPR, 25 FEB 2019, https://www.npr.org/sections/health-shots/2019/02/25/697788559/greener-childhood-associated-with-happier-adulthood

101. Ibid

102. Nadya Jones, "31 Wonderful Dry River Bed Landscaping Ideas You Will Love," A Nest With A Yard, 16 APR 2019, https://anestwithayard.com/dry-river-bed-landscaping-ideas/

103. "The State of the City Experience." Sasaki Associates@SasakiDesign, 22 JUL 2014, https://www.sasaki.com/voices/what-makes-a-city-great/

104. https://www.michelangelo.org/michelangelo-quotes.jsp

105. https://www.kyoto-art.ac.jp/en/academics/faculty/detail.php?memberId=80001

106. Jackie Carroll, Tree Topping Information – Does Tree Topping Hurt Trees, Gardening Know How, https://www.gardeningknowhow.com/ornamental/trees/tgen/tree-topping-information.htm

107. Information Report No. 194, January 1965, American Planning Association, https://www.planning.org/pas/reports/report19

108. "The Trust for Public Land ParkScore® index: The most comprehensive evaluation of park access and quality in the 100 largest U.S. cities," 2020, https://www.tpl.org/parkscore

109. "Park Acres as Percent of Land Area," City-Data Forum, 15 DEC 2009, http://www.city-data.com/forum/city-vs-city/842193-ranking-cities-most-parkland.html

110. Linda Poon, "Can Planting Trees Make a City More Equitable," Citylab Daily, 28 AUG 2020, https://www.bloomberg.com/news/newsletters/2020-08-28/citylab-daily-can-planting-trees-make-a-city-more-equitable

111. "Fire sweeps through Oakland hills," this Day in History, October 19 1991, https://www.history.com/this-day-in-history/fire-sweeps-through-oakland-hills

112. https://truenaturefoundation.org/what-is-rewilding/

113. Nathan Diller, "Trump Signs Executive Order Making 'Beautiful' The Standard For D.C.'s Federal Buildings," WAMU 88.5 American University Radio, 21 DEC 2020, https://dcist.com/story/20/12/21/trump-signs-executive-order-dc-federal-buildings-architecture/

114. Joel Garreau, "The Nine Nations of North America," Avon Books, 1982

115. Ibid

116. Boston City Hall, Wikipedia, the free encyclopedia, https://en.wikipedia.org/wiki/Boston_City_Hall

117. Mitzi J Hernandez, "18 Things You Need To Know About INTJ-Architect Personality," Thought Catalog, 25 JAN 2019, https://thoughtcatalog.com/

mitzi-j-hernandez/2019/01/18-things-you-need-to-know-about-intj-ar-chitect-personality/

118.   Daniel J. Curtin, Jr., and Cecily T. Talbert, Curtin's California Land Use and Planning Law (27th ed.) (Point Arena, CA: Solano Press, 2007).

119.   Berman v. Parker, 348 U.S. 26, 31 (1954).

120.   Novi v. City of Pacifica, 169 Cal. App. 3d 678 – Cal: Court of Appeal, 1st Appellate Dist., 5th Div., 1985.

121.   Ibid

122.   Robert Glazer, "Command and Control' Leadership Is Dead. Here's What's Taking Its Place, Hierarchical organizations with no employee autonomy or input don't work anymore. Time for a new game plan," Ink., https://www.inc.com/robert-glazer/command-control-leadership-is-dead-heres-whats-taking-its-place.html

123.   "What Are The Pros And Cons Of The Gig Economy," Forbes, 08 FEB 2019, https://www.forbes.com/sites/quora/2019/01/08/what-are-the-pros-and-cons-of-the-gig-economy/?sh=87cc41e13885

124.   "No Sweat Shakespeare," https://www.nosweatshakespeare.com/quotes/famous-shakespeare-quotes/all-the-worlds-a-stage-quote/

125.   "Animism," Wikipedia, the free encyclopedia, https://en.wikipedia.org/wiki/Animism

126.   "Belongingness Hypothesis," Psychology Concepts, http://www.psychologyconcepts.com/belongingness-hypothesis/

127.   "Unconditional love, spiritual love devoid of expectations," Spiritual Science Research Foundation, https://www.spiritualresearchfoundation.org/spiritual-practice/steps-of-spiritual-practice/spiritual-love/happiness_spirituallove_h/

128.   "What Is Spirituality?" University of Minnesota's Earl E. Bakken Center for Spirituality & Healing, https://www.takingcharge.csh.umn.edu/what-spirituality

129.   William Kent Krueger (Author), "Windigo Island: A Novel," Atria Books, August 19, 2014

130.   "Love: The Basis of Everything," The Religious A priori, https://www.doxa.ws/Theology/Love_everything.html

131.   Stuart Brown and Christopher Vaughan, Play: How It Shapes the Brain, Opens the Imagination, and Invigorates the Soul (New York: Avery, 2009).

132.   Stephen J. Suomi and Harry F. Harlow, "Monkeys Without Play," in Jerome S. Bruner, Allison Jolly, and Kathy Sylva (eds.), Play: Its Role in Development and Evolution (New York: Basic Books, 1976).

133.   Stuart Brown, "Play Deprivation... A Leading Indicator for Mass Murder," The National Institute for Play, 01 JUN 2014, http://www.nifplay.org/play-deprivation-a-leading-indicator-for-mass-murder/ Stuart Brown, "Play Deprivation... A Leading Indicator for Mass Murder," The National Institute for Play, 01 JUN 2014, http://www.nifplay.org/play-deprivation-a-leading-indicator-for-mass-murder/

134.   Editor, "19 Best Playground Games & Activities For Kids," 23 MAR 2020, https://icebreakerideas.com/playground-games/

135.   Thomas J. Gradel and Dick Simpson, "Portrait of a corrupt state," *Washington Times*, February 25, 2015, http://www.washingtontimes.com/ news/2015/feb/25/book-review-corrupt-illinois-patronage-crony-ism-an/?page=all.

136.   Fitzgerald, op. cit.

137.   First they came ..., Wikipedia, https://en.wikipedia.org/wiki/First_they_came_...

138.   https://www.worldatlas.com/articles/the-where-to-be-born-index-the-highest-and-lowest-scoring-countries.html

139.   Laura Begley Bloom, "Ranked: The 20 Happiest Countries In The World," Forbes, 20MAR2020, https://www.forbes.com/sites/laurabegley-bloom/2020/03/20/ranked-20-happiest-countries-2020/#1a8532177850

140.   "Why Scandinavian Countries Are The Happiest," Alliance Visa Ltd., https://alliancevisas.com/

141.   Naomi Blumberg, "City Beautiful movement," Encyclopædia Britannica, https://www.britannica.com/topic/City-Beautiful-movement

142.   Ibid

143.   Richard Fry, "The number of people in the average U.S. household is going up for the first time in over 160 years," Pew Research Center, 01 OCT 2019, https://www.pewresearch.org/fact-tank/2019/10/01/the-number-of-people-in-the-average-u-s-household-is-going-up-for-the-first-time-in-over-160-years/

144.   Peter Andrew, "Is Your House the 'Typical American Home," HSH Associates, Financial Publishers, 26 JAN 2020, https://www.hsh.com/home-owner/average-american-home.html

145.   Laura Mueller, "6 Reasons Why Buying a Bigger House Isn't Always a Good Idea," Move, Inc., 08 NOV 2019, https://www.moving.com/tips/6-reasons-why-buying-a-bigger-house-isnt-always-a-good-idea/

146.   Courtney Campbell, "Here's How Much Money You Need to Build Your Dream Home," HomeLight, 10 JAN 2020, https://www.homelight.com/ blog/buyer-how-much-does-it-cost-to-build-a-house/

147.   DollarTimes, H Brothers Inc, https://www.dollartimes.com/income-need-ed-for-house/200000

148.   Jay Gorney and E. Y. Harburg, "Brother, Can You Spare a Dime?" *MetroLyrics*, http://www.metrolyrics.com/brother-can-you-spare-a-dime-lyrics-bing-crosby.html.

149.   Bryce Covert, "The Government Just Took a Step Toward Ending Mass Homelessness," ThinkProgress, January 22, 2015, https://thinkprogress.org/the-government-just-took-a-step-toward-ending-mass-homelessness-c6c2bb0e9eaa/

150.   Elise Gould, The State of American Wages 2017, The Economic Policy Institute, 01 MAR 2018, https://www.epi.org/publication/the-state-of-

american-wages-2017-wages-have-finally-recovered-from-the-blow-of-the-great-recession-but-are-still-growing-too-slowly-and-unequally/#epi-toc-6

151.   Julia Horowitz, "Walmart's CEO earns 1,188 times as much as the company's median worker," CNNMoney, 23 APR 2018, https://money.cnn.com/2018/04/23/news/companies/walmart-ceo-pay/index.html

152.   "The African Americans: Many Rivers to Cross," WNET, February 7, 2015, http://www.pbs.org/wnet/african-americans-many-rivers-to-cross/

153.   Meghan Henry, Anna Mahathey, Tyler Morrill, Anna Robinson, Azim Shivji, and Rian Watt, Abt Associates, "The 2018 Annual Homeless Assessment Report to Congress," Department of Housing and Urban Development, DEC 2018.

154.   Sintia Radu, "The U.S. falls again in the annual quality-of-life assessment produced for the United Nations." U.S. News & World Report, March 20, 2019, https://www.usnews.com/news/best-countries/articles/2019-03-20/these-are-the-worlds-happiest-countries#:~:text=The%20U.S.%20ranks%20at%20No,support%20and%2042nd%20for%20corruption.

155.   Christopher Ingraham, "Americans are becoming less happy, and there's research to prove it," Washington Post, 23 MAR 2019, https://www.latimes.com/science/sciencenow/la-sci-sn-americans-less-happy-20190323-story.html

156.   "7th Generation Principle," Seven Generations International, http://7gen-foundation.org/7th-generation/

157.   https://www.mechon-mamre.org/p/pt/pt0101.htm#24

158.   Philip C.L. Gray. "Christian Stewardship: What God Expects from Us." Lay Witness, SEP 2001, https://www.catholiceducation.org/en/culture/environment/christian-stewardship-what-god-expects-from-us.html

159.   Environmental Stewardship and Conservation," The Church of Jesus Christ of Latter-day Saints, https://newsroom.churchofjesuschrist.org/article/environmental-stewardship-conservation

Chapter 3: The Limited Plan

160.   https://www.foodnetwork.com/shows/diners-drive-ins-and-dives/episodes/hearty-home-cookin

161.   Jake Blumgart, "Return to Edge City," CityLab, 10 APR 2018, https://www.bloomberg.com/news/articles/2018-04-10/what-edge-city-got-right-and-wrong-about-america

162.   "Trenchless technology," Wikipedia, https://en.wikipedia.org/wiki/Trenchless_technology

163.   Jorge L. Ortiz, "Drive the plastic highway? How a California company's innovative repaving process could lead to the 'holy grail' of road construction," USA TODAY, 10 AUG 2020, https://www.msn.com/en-us/news/technology/plastic-water-and-soda-bottles-are-being-recycled-into-a-new-highway-in-california/ar-BB17J5Cs

164.   "The Abbey of Montecassino." Tour of Italy for the Financially Challenged/
       touritaly.org, http://www.touritaly.org/tours/montecassino/cassino01.htm

165.   John Ezard, "Error led to bombing of Monte Cassino Monastery destroyed
       after translation slip by British intelligence officer," The Guardian, 03 APR
       2000, https://www.theguardian.com/world/2000/apr/04/johnezard

166.   The Secretary of the Interior's Standards for the Treatment of Historic Prop-
       erties with Guidelines for Preserving, Rehabilitating, Restoring & Recon-
       structing Historic Buildings, U.S. Department of the Interior National
       Park Service Technical Preservation Services, https://www.nps.gov/tps/
       standards/treatment-guidelines-2017.pdf

167.   "State Highway Types," CALTRANS, https://www.cahighways.org/stypes.
       html

168.   John Urgo, Meredith Wilensky, and Steven Weissman, *Moving Beyond Pre-
       vailing Street Design Standards: Assessing Legal and Liability Barriers to More
       Efficient Street Design and Function* (Berkeley: University of California,
       2011). Accessed July 11, 2019, https://www.law.berkeley.edu/files/4.1_
       CREC_codes_and_standards.pdf

169.   Ibid

170.   "Neighborhood Streets Project Stakeholders, Neighborhood Street Design
       Guidelines: An Oregon Guide for Reducing Street Widths, Stakeholder
       Design Team," 2000,

171.   https://www.oregon.gov/lcd/Publications/NeighborhoodStreetDe-
       sign_2000.pdf   "Merriam-Webster Legal Dictionary," Merriam-Webster
       Inc., https://www.merriam-webster.com/legal/reasonable%20person

172.   Frank Alonso and Carolyn A. E. Greenwell, "Underground vs. Overhead:
       Power Line Installation-Cost Comparison and Mitigation," POWERGEN
       International,   01   FEB   2013,https://www.power-grid.com/td/under-
       ground-vs-overhead-power-line-installation-cost-comparison/

173.   Frank Alonso and Carolyn A. E. Greenwell, SAIC, "Underground vs.
       Overhead: Power Line Installation-Cost Comparison and Mitigation,"
       Power   Grid   International,   https://www.power-grid.com/2013/02/01/
       underground-vs-overhead-power-line-installation-cost-comparison/

174.   https://www.playlsi.com/en/playground-planning-tools/education/

175.   Lucia, "Desert Dwellings: How to Design for the Desert," Modlar, 2016,
       https://www.modlar.com/news/180/desert-dwellings-how-to-design-for-
       the-desert/

176.   Berkeley Disability Access & Compliance," UC Berkley, https://dac.
       berkeley.edu/wurster-hall

177.   https://file.lacounty.gov/SDSInter/lac/1043530_09-10CitiesAlpha.pdf

178.   "Revolutionizing recycling at the molecular level: Eastman begins commer-
       cial operation of innovative chemical recycling technology," 23 OCT 2019,
       https://www.eastman.com/Company/News_Center/2019/Pages/East-
       man-begins-commercial-operation-of-innovative-chemical-recycling-tech-
       nology.aspx

179. Frank Newport, "Americans Big on Idea of Living in the Country," Gallup, 07 DEC 2018, https://news.gallup.com/poll/245249/americans-big-idea-living-country.aspx

180. "10 tallest buildings in the world," Architecture, 21 OCT 2019 https://www.cnn.com/style/article/tallest-buildings-world-2019/index.html

181. Economic Research Service www.ers.usda.govUnited States Department of Agriculture Bigelow, Daniel P., and Allison Borchers, "Major Uses of Land in the United States, 2012,EIB-178, U.S. Department of Agriculture, Economic Research Service, AUG 2017

182. https://stats.oecd.org/Index.aspx?DataSetCode=BLI

183. Ibid

184. Dalai Lama, "What is the Purpose of Life," GoodReads,13 JUL 2020, https://www.goodreads.com/quotes/401282-i-believe-that-the-very-purpose-of-life-is-to

185. "Human sense of fairness evolved to favor long-term cooperation, primate study suggests," ScienceDaily, Georgia State University, September 18, 2014, https://www.sciencedaily.com/releases/2014/09/140918141151.htm

186. Sean Markey, "Monkeys Show Sense of Fairness, Study Says," National Geographic News, October 28, 2010, http://news.nationalgeographic.com/ news/2003/09/0917_030917_monkeyfairness.html/. The experiment was con- ducted by Dr. Sarah Brosnan, of Georgia State University Departments of Psychology and Philosophy, and Dr. Frans de Waal, of the Yerkes National Primate Research Center and the Psychology Department at Emory University.

187. Brentin Mock, "Why Detroit Residents Pushed Back Against Tree-Planting," Bloomberg CityLab, 11 JAN 2019, https://www.bloomberg.com/news/articles/2019-01-11/why-detroiters-didn-t-trust-city-tree-planting-efforts

188. Amy Fontinelle, "Standard of Living vs. Quality of Life: What's the Difference?" Investopedia, 21 JUL 2020, https://www.investopedia.com/articles/financial-theory/08/standard-of-living-quality-of-life.asp

189. Brett Kelman and Jesse Marx, "DA: Former Beaumont officials siphoned $43 million," The Desert Sun, May 18, 2016, http://www.desertsun.com/story/news/crime_courts/2016/05/17/six-beaumont-officials-charged-embezzlement/84500932/.

190. "Leadership Training," National League of Cities, https://www.nlc.org/resources-training/nlc-university/

191. "Planning Commissions and Boards," APA American Planning Association, https://www.planning.org/online-education/

192. Laura Begley Bloom, "20 Happiest And 20 Unhappiest Cities In America," ForbesWomen, 12 MAR 2019, https://www.forbes.com/sites/laurabegleybloom/2019/03/12/20-happiest-and-20-unhappiest-cities-in-america/#3275e6063a70

193. "Plano, Texas," Wikipedia, https://en.wikipedia.org/wiki/Plano,_Texas

194. "Decline of Detroit," Wikipedia, https://en.wikipedia.org/wiki/Decline_of_Detroit

195. "Santa Clara Swim Club," Wikipedia, https://en.wikipedia.org/wiki/Santa_Clara_Swim_Club

Chapter 4: The Specific Plan

196. Jarrett Walker, basics: walking distance to transit, Human Transit, 24 APR 2011, https://humantransit.org/2011/04/basics-walking-distance-to-transit.html

197. Metes and bounds, Wikipedia, the free encyclopedia, https://en.wikipedia.org/wiki/Metes_and_bounds

198. "AP US: Growth Of America (c. 1800 - 1860)," https://apwiki.wikidot.com/ap-us:growth-of-america

199. Mike Maciag, "Population Density for U.S. Cities Statistics," Governing, 29 NOV 2017 https://www.governing.com/gov-data/population-density-land-area-cities-map.html

200. "Form-Based Codes Defined," Form-Based Codes Institute, https://formbasedcodes.org/definition/

201. Daniel G. Parolek, AIA, Karen Parolek, Paul C. Crawford, FAICP, "Form Based Codes: A Guide for Planners, Urban Designers, Municipalities, and Developers," Wiley, http://www.wiley.com/WileyCDA/WileyTitle/productCd-0470049855.html

202. "Form-Based Codes Defined," https://formbasedcodes.org/definition/

Chapter 5: The Emergency Plan

203. Maggie Gordon, "Repeat flooding has residents asking: Is Houston worth it," Houston Chronicle, 23 SEP 2019, https://www.houstonchronicle.com/news/houston-texas/houston/article/Repeat-flooding-has-residents-asking-Is-Houston-14456965.php

204. Delilah Friedler, "California's Wildfire Policy Totally Backfired." Mother Jones,11NOV2019, https://www.motherjones.com/environment/2019/11/californias-wildfire-controlled-prescribed-burns-native-americans/

205. Chuck DeVore, "Wildfires Caused By Bad Environmental Policy Are Causing California Forests To Be Net CO2 Emitters," Forbes Magazine, 25 FEB 2019, https://www.forbes.com/sites/chuckdevore/2019/02/25/wildfires-caused-by-bad-environmental-policy-are-causing-california-forests-to-be-net-co2-emitters/#4fddd9b55e30

Chapter 6: Applied Planning

206.   http://www.sanfrancisco.com/neighborhoods/

207.   http://en.wikipedia.org/wiki/Category:Neighborhoods_in_Los_Angeles,_California

208.   Size of Chinese Family Getting Smaller, China Daily, http://www.china-daily.com.cn/china/2014-05/15/content_17508456.htm

209.   https://www.researchgate.net/publication/235356904_Sense_of_Community_A_Definition_and_Theory

210.   National Center for Safe Routes to School, accessed, May 16, 2015, http://www.saferoutesinfo.org/program-tools/what-distances-are-reasonable-expect-elementary-school-students-bike-school

211.   "Mapping LA Neighborhoods," latimes.com http://maps.latimes.com/neighborhoods/neighborhood/list/

212.   Revised Code of Washington (RCW) Title 39 > Chapter 39.88 > Section 39.88.100, https://apps.leg.wa.gov/RCW/default.aspx?cite=39.88.100

Chapter 7: The Redevelopment Plan

213.   "Prime Directive," Wikipedia, http://en.wikipedia.org/wiki/Prime_Directive.

214.   "Gresham's law," Wikipedia, https://en.wikipedia.org/wiki/Gresham%27s_law.

215.   In the Matter of Condemnation by Urban Redevelopment Authority, 117 Pa. Commonwealth Ct. 475 (1988), 544 A.2d 87, https://law.justia.com/cases/pennsylvania/commonwealth-court/1988/117-pa-commw-475-0.html

216.   "Minnesota Tax Increment Financing Glossary," Minnesota House of Representatives, House Research Department, http://www.house.leg.state.mn.us/hrd/issinfo/tif/gloss.aspx#l1.

217.   CRA/LA [successor to the Community Redevelopment Agency of the City of Los Angeles, California], http://www.crala.org/internet-site/index.cfm.

218.   "Public Nuisance" The free dictionary by Farlex, Inc, https://legal-dictionary.thefreedictionary.com/public+nuisance

219.   Abraham H. Maslow, A Theory of Human Motivation, Martino Fine Books, June 12, 2013

220.   Josh Clark, "Why do we love?" HowStuffWorks, http://people.howstuffworks.com/why-do-we-love.htm.

221.   Jeremy Rozansky, "San Bernardino's Route to Bankruptcy," City Journal, 18JUL2012, http://www.city-journal.org/2012/cjc0718jr.html.

222.   "Redevelopment Wrecks: 20 Failed Projects Involving Eminent Domain Abuse," The Castle Coalition, http://castlecoalition.org/pdf/publications/Redevelopment%20Wrecks.pdf.

223. "Redevelopment Wrecks: Indio, CA," The Castle Coalition, JUN 2006, http://castlecoalition.org/redevelopment-wrecks-indio

224. APA Policy Guide on Public Redevelopment, 25APR2004, https://www.planning.org/policy/guides/adopted/redevelopment.htm

225. David Barboza, Chicago, Offering Big Incentives, Will Be Boeing's New Home, New York Times, 11MAY2001, https://www.nytimes.com/2001/05/11/business/chicago-offering-big-incentives-will-be-boeings-new-home.html

226. "Controller Issues Redevelopment Findings," California State Controller's Office, 03MAR2011, http://www.sco.ca.gov/eo_pressrel_9789.html.

227. "Audit faults California redevelopment agencies," recordnet.com, 07 MAR 2011, https://www.recordnet.com/article/20110307/A_NEWS/110309918

228. Maura Dolan, Jessica Garrison, and Anthony York, "California high court puts redevelopment agencies out of business," Los Angeles Times, 29DEC2011, http://articles.latimes.com/2011/dec/29/local/la-me-redevelopment-20111230.

229. "Field of Dreams," Wikiquote, https://en.wikiquote.org/wiki/Field_of_Dreams.

Chapter 8: The Preservation Plan

230. "Painted ladies," Wikipedia, https://en.wikipedia.org/wiki/Painted_ladies

231. Chris Moon and Madison Miller, "How Long Do Homeowners Stay in Their Homes?" ValuePenguin, 04 JUN 2018, https://www.valuepenguin.com/how-long-homeowners-stay-in-their-homes

232. Jason Barry, City of Glendale defends decision to sell downtown building for $25,000, AZFamily, A Meredith Corporation Station, 10OCT2018 https://www.azfamily.com/news/city-of-glendale-defends-decision-to-sell-downtown-building-for-25-000/article_ba31ef7a-cce3-11e8-816b-ab82616925e0.html

233. Bobby Azarian Ph.D., "A Complete Psychological Analysis of Trump's Support," Psychology Today, 27 DEC 2018, https://www.psychologytoday.com/us/blog/mind-in-the-machine/201812/complete-psychological-analysis-trumps-support

234. Joseph W. Kane and Adie Tomer, "Shifting into an era of repair: US infrastructure spending trends," The Brookings Institution, 10 MAY 2019, https://www.brookings.edu/research/shifting-into-an-era-of-repair-us-infrastructure-spending-trends/

235. Storper, "Blanket Upzoning Blunt Instrument Won't Solve Affordable Housing Crisis," The Planning Report, 15 MAR 2019, https://www.planningreport.com/2019/03/15/blanket-upzoning-blunt-instrument-wont-solve-affordable-housing-crisis

236. "Standard Garage Size Dimensions for 1,2,3,4 Car Garages," Epic Home

Ideas an online magazine, https://www.epichomeideas.com/standard-garage-size-dimensions/#:~:text=%20Here%20are%20the%20standard%20dimensions%3A%20%201,door%20widths%20are%20between%20 7-9%20feet.%20More%20

237. Andrew Lee, "What Is Gentrification? How It Works, Who It Affects, and What to Do About It," Teen Vogue, 20 OCT 2020, https://www.teen-vogue.com/story/what-is-gentrification-how-works

238. Ibid

239. Ibid

240. Ibid

241. "Household income in the United States," Wikipedia, https://en.wikipedia.org/wiki/Household_income_in_the_United_States

242. "Exploring Upzoning as a Tool to Increase California's Housing Supply," Terner Center for Housing Innovation and Urban Displacement Project, University of California, Berkeley, http://upzoning.berkeley.edu/

243. Pete Saunders, "Maybe Upzoning Doesn't (Always) Lead To Lower Home Prices," Forbs Magazine, 22 FEB 2019https://www.forbes.com/sites/petesaunders1/2019/02/22/maybe-upzoning-doesnt-always-lead-to-lower-home-prices/?sh=65db9ada4dd3

244. Jenny Schuetz, "Minneapolis 2040: The most wonderful plan of the year," The Brookings Institution, 12 DEC 2018, https://www.brookings.edu/blog/the-avenue/2018/12/12/minneapolis-2040-the-most-wonderful-plan-of-the-year/

245. Prableen Bajpai, "The 5 Largest Economies In The World And Their Growth In 2020," Nasdaq, Inc., 22 JAN 2020, https://www.nasdaq.com/articles/the-5-largest-economies-in-the-world-and-their-growth-in-2020-2020-01-22

246. Greg Leiserson, Will McGrew, Raksha Kopparam, "The distribution of wealth in the United States and implications for a net worth tax," The Washington Center for Equitable Growth, 21 MAR 2019, https://equitablegrowth.org/the-distribution-of-wealth-in-the-united-states-and-implications-for-a-net-worth-tax/

247. "SuperValu TidyTowns Competition," Department of Rural and Community Development, https://www.tidytowns.ie/

Chapter 9: You Make a Difference

248. "It's a Wonderful Life (1946)," https://www.imdb.com/title/tt0038650/

249. VisionPDX, http://www.visionpdx.com/

250. VisionPDX, "Urban Livability," http://www.visionpdx.com/reading/inputsummary/urban_livability/index.html

251. Emily Badger, "The Shopping Mall Turns 60 (and Prepares to Retire)," City Lab, July 13, 2012, http://www.citylab.com/design/2012/07/shopping-mall-turns-60-and-prepares-retire/2568/

252. Ibid

253. https://www.quora.com/Why-is-Mountain-View-so-different-from-Sunnyvale-Sunnyvale-seems-to-be-an-endless-expanse-of-chain-stores-while-Mountain-View-has-a-bit-of-its-own-character?share=1

254. "Public Participation Guide: Process Planning, Step 1. Organize for Participation," US Environmental Protection Agency, http://www2.epa.gov/international-cooperation/public-participation-guide-process-planning#-step1.

255. Ibid

256. Michael J. Sandel, What Money Can't Buy: The Moral Limits of Markets (New York: Farrar Straus and Giroux, 2013).

257. Doyle Rice, "US, world population to shrink after midcentury, study suggests," USA Today, 14 JUL 2020, https://www.usatoday.com/story/news/nation/2020/07/14/lancet-study-us-world-population-shrink-after-midcentury/5434571002/

258. Anthony Cilluffo and Neil G. Ruiz, "World's population is projected to nearly stop growing by the end of the century," Pew Research Center, 17 JUN 2019, https://www.pewresearch.org/fact-tank/2019/06/17/worlds-population-is-projected-to-nearly-stop-growing-by-the-end-of-the-century/

259. "Best Countries for Business 2018 - Mexico," Forbes, https://www.forbes.com/places/mexico/?sh=6955417e4b2d

260. "Happy Planet Index," New Economics Foundation, http://happyplanetindex.org/countries/mexico/

261. Economic Research Service www.ers.usda.govUnited States Department of Agriculture Bigelow, Daniel P., and Allison Borchers, "Major Uses of Land in the United States, 2012,EIB-178, U.S. Department of Agriculture, Economic Research Service, AUG 2017

262. Economic Research Service www.ers.usda.govUnited States Department of Agriculture Bigelow, Daniel P., and Allison Borchers, "Major Uses of Land in the United States, 2012,EIB-178, U.S. Department of Agriculture, Economic Research Service, AUG 2017

263. "A Current Inventory of Vacant Urban Land in America," Journal of Urban Design 21(3):302-319, MAY2016, https://www.researchgate.net/publication/301490995_A_Current_Inventory_of_Vacant_Urban_Land_in_America

264. Dusty Ferguson, "These Places in the US Are Giving Out FREE Land in 2020," dimewilltell,10APR 2020, https://dimewilltell.com/free-land/

265. Marlow Vester, Ralph E. Heimlich, and Kenneth S. Krupa. "Urbanization of Rural Land in the United States." Resources and Technology Division, Economic Research Service, U.S. Department of Agriculture. Agricultural Economic Report No.673. https://naldc.nal.usda.gov/download/CAT10662990/PDF

266.   Adam McCann, "2020's Fastest-Growing Cities in America," WalletHub,12 OCT 2020, https://wallethub.com/edu/fastest-growing-cities/7010

267.   "Fastest-Growing Places in the U.S. in 2020-21," U.S. News & World Report L.P., https://realestate.usnews.com/places/rankings/fastest-growing-places"Fastest-Growing Places in the U.S. in 2020-21," U.S. News & World Report L.P., https://realestate.usnews.com/places/rankings/fastest-growing-places

268.   Scott Mautz, "A 2-Year Stanford Study Shows the Astonishing Productivity Boost of Working From Home," INC., https://www.inc.com/scott-mautz/a-2-year-stanford-study-shows-astonishing-productivity-boost-of-working-from-home.html

269.   Stephen J. Suomi and Harry F. Harlow, "Monkeys Without Play," in Jerome S. Bruner, Allison Jolly, and Kathy Sylva (eds.), Play: Its Role in Development and Evolution (New York: Basic Books, 1976).

270.   https://www.wework.com/

271.   Aaron Bialick, "How Friedel Klussmann Saved the Cable Cars 70 Years Ago," San Francisco Municipal Transportation Agency (SFMTA). All rights rese   26 JAN 2017 https://www.sfmta.com/blog/how-friedel-klussmann-saved-cable-cars-70-years-ago